HIDDEN
HISTORY
of
MISHAWAKA

HIDDEN
HISTORY
of
MISHAWAKA

Peter J. De Kever

THE
History
PRESS

Published by The History Press
Charleston, SC
www.historypress.com

First published 2021

Manufactured in the United States

ISBN 9781467148917

Library of Congress Control Number: 2021943820

Notice: The information in this book is true and complete to the best of our knowledge. It is offered without guarantee on the part of the author or The History Press. The author and The History Press disclaim all liability in connection with the use of this book.

CONTENTS

1. First Mayor of the City of Mishawaka:
   The Life of Manuel Fisher 7
2. A Rousing Reception:
   Vice President Fairbanks Visits Mishawaka 22
3. One Glorious Day:
   Mishawaka's Independence Day Celebration of 1909 36
4. Picturing History: Mishawaka Recruits and World War I 55
5. A Stall in the Cow Barn: The Mishawaka Cavemen
   and the 1927 Basketball State Finals 69
6. Mishawaka's Battleground: Celebrating the Eightieth Anniversary
   of Steele Stadium's WPA Bleachers 89
7. Mishawaka High School Football's Twenty Greatest
   Home Wins, 1939–2018 106
8. From Mishawaka to Tokyo: Ball-Band and
   the Doolittle Raid 115
9. The Mishawakan Who Saved Ford Motor Company:
   Richard Caleal and the 1949 Ford 131
10. Mishawaka Strikes Back: Bendix's Talos Missile
    and the Vietnam War 144

About the Author 159

FIRST MAYOR OF THE CITY OF MISHAWAKA

The Life of Manuel Fisher

On January 2, 2020, Robert Beutter, a former mayor of Mishawaka, passed away. "Mayor Bob" was Mishawaka's nineteenth mayor, part of a line of leaders stretching back to the nineteenth century. Other mayors' names once known in every Mishawaka household have faded into the haze of history, including the city's first mayor, Manuel M. Fisher.

Manuel was born in Williams Center, Ohio, on August 8, 1848, the eldest of Phillip and Lydia Fisher's three children. The unincorporated village of Williams Center is located four miles southwest of Bryan, the Williams County seat, in the northwest corner of Ohio.

According to the 1850 U.S. Census, Phillip, then age thirty-one, was a native of Pennsylvania and worked as a "carpenter and joiner." Lydia, eight years younger, was born in Virginia. The Fishers' daughter, Nettie, was born three years after Manuel, and another son died at age five in 1868. Charles Chapman's *History of St. Joseph County, Indiana*, published in 1880, states that Manuel grew up on a farm and attended the common school and normal high school of Bryan.

When the Civil War began in April 1861, Manuel was twelve years old. For the next four years, he watched neighbors and friends head off to war, and he heard and read about the martial exploits of Ohioans at battles such as Shiloh and Gettysburg. When Fisher was just shy of sixteen and a half years old, he enlisted in Company A of the 189th Ohio Volunteer Infantry Regiment on January 6, 1865. The regiment was formed at Camp

Chase in Columbus, 130 miles southeast of Williams County.

The 189th Ohio was mustered into service on March 5, 1865; departed Camp Chase two days later for Huntsville, Alabama; and arrived on March 17. The major fighting in that part of the Confederacy was over by then, and the 189th was relegated to guarding bridges and constructing stockades. Seven of its companies were positioned along a sixty-seven-mile stretch of the Memphis & Charleston Railroad between Decatur, southwest of Huntsville, and Stevenson to the northeast. By June 20, the regiment was concentrated at Huntsville, where it was on post duty.

MANUEL M. FISHER.

Manuel Fisher. *Mishawaka-Penn-Harris Public Library.*

During its service, the 189th Ohio had one enlisted man killed, but the greater peril it faced was disease, which claimed forty-eight men. Letters sent home and published in the *Toledo Blade* reported that the Ohioans were also suffering from homesickness and "the monotony of camp" and frequently asking, "When are we going home?"

That question was soon answered for Private Fisher and his comrades. On September 25, the regiment was ordered to Nashville, Tennessee, where it stayed until mustered out of service on September 28. The 189th returned to Camp Chase, and Manuel was discharged on October 7, 1865.

According to *South Bend and Mishawaka*, a history published in 1901, Fisher's health had "become impaired," perhaps from his military service. In the 1870 U.S. Census, twenty-two-year-old Manuel was living with his parents and sister in Bryan, and his profession was "school teacher."

That year, Fisher moved eighty-five miles west to Mishawaka, where he was hired as a laborer by Palmer "P.C." Perkins, who had opened P.C. Perkins & Company the previous year. The business produced edge tools, pumps and water tanks but primarily manufactured Perkins Wind Mills, which P.C. had invented and patented. He then formed a partnership with his twin brother, Pardon, and incorporated as Perkins Wind Mill & Ax Company in 1873. Known for its windmills' simple design and ease of maintenance, Perkins grew steadily in the following decades and was producing five thousand windmills annually by 1899, filling orders from throughout the United States and internationally.

Fisher was president and superintendent of Perkins Wind Mill Company, one of Mishawaka's great industries. The factory is shown here, circa 1907. *Mishawaka-Penn-Harris Public Library.*

Fisher joined P.C. Perkins & Company soon after its beginning and worked his way up to foreman and shipping clerk and then superintendent before also becoming company president in 1896.

At the same time Manuel was helping Perkins's rise, he entered into marriage and started a family. On December 24, 1871, he married twenty-one-year-old Elizabeth Miller, who was a native of Hicksville, Ohio, located twelve miles southwest of Williams Center. Libbie and her parents had moved to Mishawaka in 1868.

When Elizabeth gave birth to the couple's first child, Bonnie, on May 26, 1874, the *Mishawaka Enterprise* reported the event in two articles. Under the headline "A Successful Fisher," editor Edward Jernegan playfully noted that "M.M. Fisher, foreman of the Perkins Wind Mill & Ax Co., caught a 10-pound girl last Monday." Another article stated that workers at the factory "were much pleased" by Fisher "bringing in a box of cigars and telling them that it was a girl and weighed ten pounds."

On May 13, 1878, Manuel and Elizabeth's joy turned to sorrow when Bonnie died. "Mr. and Mrs. M.M. Fisher have been sorely afflicted this week in the loss of their only child, a lovely little girl of four years," stated the *Enterprise*. "The bereaved parents have the universal sympathy of our citizens in their sorrow." Bonnie was buried in the Miller family's plot at City Cemetery in South Bend. The Fishers would have no other children.

In addition to his family life and professional obligations, Manuel was heavily involved in his church and various groups and fraternal organizations. He joined the First Presbyterian Church in 1870, was superintendent of its Sunday school for twenty-five years and was an elder. Chapman's *History* described Manuel as "a zealous worker in the cause of temperance." He served as worshipful master of the Mishawaka lodge of the Masons, high priest of the Mishawaka chapter of the Royal Arch Masons, eminent commander of the South Bend chapter and grand captain and grand high priest of the Royal Arch Masons of Indiana. Fisher also belonged to the Knights Templar and Odd Fellows, and he was commander of Houghton Post No. 128 of the Grand Army of the Republic.

In 1895, Manuel also helped organize a company that would establish an electric light plant for Mishawaka.

Manuel and Libbie resided in an attractive two-story, woodframe house at 222 East Second Street (Lincolnway). It is unknown when the Fishers moved to that location. According to a Sanborn Map Company publication from March 1886, another house stood there, but an aerial illustration of Mishawaka in 1890 and a July 1891 Sanborn map show the house where the Fishers lived when he was elected mayor. Within a block of the Fishers resided some of Mishawaka's most prominent citizens, a short walk from downtown and their businesses. One house to the west was owned by James Roper, president of Roper Furniture Company, and across the street were the homes of Martin Beiger, president of Mishawaka Woolen Company, and Ed Jernegan. One block east and on the north side of the street, Frederick Eberhart Jr. and Everett Eberhart, both executives at Mishawaka Woolen, had their residences. The homes of Reuben Perkins, secretary and treasurer of Perkins Wind Mill Company, and Hattie Dodge, the widow of Dodge Manufacturing Company founder Wallace Dodge, were across the street.

Through his leadership role at Perkins and various forms of community involvement, Manuel earned the respect of his fellow townspeople, as stated in *South Bend and Mishawaka*: "Mr. Fisher is widely known and esteemed in every walk of life and is a gentleman of resolute character, quick in action, firm in the defense of right, and a man of the people." Such a reputation made a career in elected public service a natural fit for Manuel, who served on the town board for five years and was its president for two years.

In February 1899, Mishawaka voters again took up the momentous question of whether to change their government from a town to a city. In 1871 and 1896, they had addressed this matter and decided to keep the town form of governance that dated to 1835. After much politicking and

Manuel Fisher and his wife resided at 222 East Second Street. *Mishawaka-Penn-Harris Public Library.*

debating, the Mishawaka electorate voted by a 702-336 margin to adopt a city charter. The *Enterprise* of February 24 memorably personified the election's result: "The third time proved the charm, and at Monday's special election Mishawaka voted to cast off her outgrown and antiquated baby clothes and don the more appropriate and up-to-date habiliments of municipal manhood."

The change to city government meant that the old town board would be replaced by a ten-member city council, with two councilmen being elected from each of five newly drawn wards. The city charter also established an elected office of mayor. Mishawaka voters would elect the mayor, councilmen, clerk, treasurer and marshal on May 2.

On April 14, the Republicans held a convention in a packed city hall, located above the waterworks on North Church Street, to determine their slate of nominees. Fifty-five delegates considered three candidates for mayor: Manuel Fisher, Melville Mix and William Miller. Mix was president of Dodge Manufacturing, and Miller, son of a former mayor of South Bend, was manager, secretary and treasurer of Mishawaka Paper & Pulp Company. Fisher led Mix and Miller through the first five ballots, after which Miller withdrew and Fisher won the nomination on the sixth ballot, 29-23. Miller then moved to make the nomination unanimous, a motion affirmed with a shout by the assemblage, which called for Manuel to speak. According to

During the Fisher administration, city council meetings were held on the second floor of the waterworks building on North Church Street. *Mishawaka-Penn-Harris Public Library.*

the *Enterprise* account, Fisher "made a brief speech of acknowledgment for the honor conferred and promised, if elected, to devote his best and most earnest efforts for the good of Mishawaka."

In the same article that reported on the nomination convention, Republican Ed Jernegan offered his favorable assessment: "Mr. Fisher, it is conceded by all, will make a most efficient and energetic mayor." Jernegan noted Manuel's "unimpeachable" record as a town trustee in which he demonstrated "force and intelligence." The endorsement also predicted that Fisher's experience leading a large corporation would make him well suited for the challenges of being the city's first mayor.

One day after the Republicans' convention, it was Mishawaka Democrats' turn to fill city hall. They nominated E. Volney Bingham, a prominent attorney and former state senator, for mayor.

After Mishawakans went to the polls, Manuel Fisher and his fellow Republicans were celebrating an impressive triumph. Fisher defeated Bingham, 656-612, and the Republicans took the clerk, treasurer and marshal contests. They also claimed six of the ten council seats. The *Enterprise* asserted that the "sweeping victory" was a "tremendous surprise" to the Democrats, who believed that Bingham was "invincible" and that they would control the council. "It was a Republican day, and the fates were with us," Jernegan concluded.

When the election returns indicated a Republican win, GOP supporters took to the streets, shouting and setting off firecrackers. Mayor-elect Fisher and other victorious candidates handed out cigars to the crowd of enthusiastic well-wishers.

The pro-Republican *South Bend Tribune* also applauded the election's outcome: "Republicans of Mishawaka, all hail! You have done nobly. You have started the new city on a right course; you are deserving of great praise. The election of your entire city ticket and a majority of the councilmanic candidates is certainly a victory of which you may well feel proud." The *Tribune* wrote approvingly of Manuel Fisher, who was "acknowledged by all to be as good a man as the town afforded for the place. He is a representative citizen in the fullest sense of the term, and his name added strength to the ticket."

With the exciting campaign and election over, it was time to get down to the business of governing. First, though, an extraordinary moment in the history of Mishawaka politics took place in the city council chambers on the evening of May 8, 1899. In front of "100 leading citizens…including three pastors of local churches," the *Tribune* described, the old town board met for the last time. It heard an official statement on the recent elections, accepted a report on the town's finances and burned the canceled bonds and paid coupons from the previous year. After this regular business was concluded, the board adjourned and, after sixty-four years, ceased to exist.

Newly elected city officials were then sworn in, the council elected William Hosford as president pro tem and bonds were set for the mayor, clerk and marshal's salaries. The *Enterprise* account describes the historic moment that followed: "Councilman Hosford then escorted Mr. Fisher to the chair amid the ringing applause of the attending spectators and presented the first mayor of Mishawaka to the council and the city."

Mayor Fisher read his inaugural address, which both the *Enterprise* and *Tribune* reprinted in its entirety. Addressing his "fellow citizens of Mishawaka," Fisher began by reviewing the recent political tumult over whether Mishawaka should remain a town or become a city. Invoking the example of President William McKinley's expansionist policy after the previous year's Spanish-American War, the mayor asserted that "the citizens of Mishawaka have been imbued with the same idea, that our beautiful town was worthy of more than the name of incorporation." After the February

20 election decided the matter, he explained, Mishawakans turned to the issue of "which party should direct the laying of the foundation stones upon which our future structure should rest for all time to come." Fisher characterized the results of the May 2 election as divinely directed: "He who maketh a nation to rise and fall in a day, had mapped out for us a more progressive spirit."

After indulging in a moment of partisan celebration, Mayor Fisher urged that "the first officers of the city of Mishawaka endeavor to do our whole duty. Looking beyond the narrow confines of self and party, let us endeavor to make Mishawaka what it should be."

Fisher proceeded to share his vision for Mishawaka with stirring eloquence:

> *While we are not a city set on a hill, let us not hide in the beautiful valley in which we are situated; but let us strive by the foundations which we as officers lay, to build up for her a more noble heritage.*
>
> *Today Mishawaka, as a town, is known all over the civilized world. Her manufactures have made her famous. Her goods are used in every clime. Many of her products are household words, and those who have ever lived any length of time in her narrow confines, if called upon to locate elsewhere as did Daniel, the captive, in olden times, look with longing eyes toward this, their beacon light, and their expectation is that they will return to the land of their fathers.*
>
> *So let us endeavor to keep pace or, better, to forge ahead with the true expansive spirit, making public improvements, within our means, that will tend to make their streets more tractable; making such laws that the morals of our city may be improved, and doing our utmost to impress upon all that laws of country, state, and city must be honored.*

Referring to city officials as "fellow laborers," the mayor called on them to "labor for the city's advancement" and to "guard the city's capital entrusted to our care…as if it were our own."

Fisher then asked Mishawaka citizens for their assistance in this labor, urging them to "take an interest in your city's welfare" and "willingly devote your time and talents…to build up our beautiful city" in a "spirit of self-sacrifice" so that "peace and harmony prevail."

As the mayor neared the speech's end, his comments became more personal. Fisher expressed his gratitude, "especially to you laboring men, who possess the brawn and sinew of our city," for electing him "first mayor of the city of Mishawaka." He also promised to carry out his duties in such a manner that "not one of you will ever regret the choice you have made." Fisher then stated that his "earnest desire [was] to administer a just government 'of the people, for the people.'" While pledging to "always strive to please you in your desires and regards so far as my power lies," he also cautioned citizens to "expect many delays and hindrances" and to understand that limited municipal finances would not permit "all that you may desire." Mayor Fisher also vowed "to see that no injustice is done to those who are helpless," to be mindful of "the interests of all concerned" and to ensure that national, state and city laws "be faithfully kept."

Fisher concluded the address by urging city officials to show fidelity to their responsibilities and added, "May peace and harmony prevail within our ranks, and may the scale of justice, 'do to others as you would that they should do to you,' be our motto."

In its first items of business, the new council elected a city attorney, fire chief and officers of the board of health. A council committee on salaries was appointed, and the longtime caretaker of Battell Park was retained.

The *Tribune*'s observer was impressed by how Fisher handled the meeting: "Mayor Fisher took charge of the executive body in an easy and dignified manner and at once showed his ability as a parliamentarian and executive officer."

In its account of the evening, the *Enterprise* noted that Manuel's friends from South Bend had given two "magnificent" floral table displays, one of which was a large mound of ferns and hundreds of red and white roses resting on an American flag. After the council meeting adjourned, the mayor "distributed many of the roses as souvenirs of the occasion."

A remarkable artifact from this first city council meeting survives today in a vault at city hall. A large ledger book labeled as Book 1 of the City of Mishawaka's records has a handwritten paragraph listing the names and offices of all the new councilmen, mayor, clerk, treasurer and marshal. The text of their oath of office is then stated, followed by each man's signature.

Among the issues to decide at the first full council meeting on May 26 were hiring staff, such as a city engineer, and establishing salaries for the mayor, marshal, clerk, city attorney and fire chief. The committee tasked with this matter recommended a $300 annual salary for the mayor, but Fisher proposed that this amount be lowered by $100 and added to the marshal's pay, which would be increased to $600. The council approved the mayor's request. Mayor Fisher, who continued to be president of Perkins Wind Mill Company, did not need the money but was eager to selflessly serve his city, despite the challenges inherent to the office.

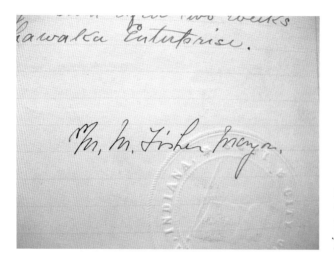

Mayor Fisher signed the ordinance approving a city board of health on June 26, 1899. *Author's collection.*

Early city council meetings established other precedents and procedures for the new city government. For example, at its June 26 meeting, the council adopted an ordinance creating a board of health. A handwritten version of the document covers several pages of the city record book, followed by the signature, "M.M. Fisher Mayor."

City business during Fisher's three-year term largely involved managing finances and infrastructure, such as streets, sewers, the electric plant and the waterworks. This task was made all the more difficult as Mishawaka's industries expanded and the city's population boomed. At nearly every council meeting, citizens were petitioning for extending streets, sewers, water lines or streetlights. *South Bend and Mishawaka* asserts, "During his regime, most extensive paving, sewer, and lighting improvements have been made in an economical way."

Eight months after Manuel took office, his father, Phillip, died on January 10, 1900. Phillip and Lydia still resided in Bryan but had come to Mishawaka for Thanksgiving. The elder Fisher had been attending a service at the Baptist church when he became seriously ill. Phillip was then taken to Manuel and Libbie's home, but doctors' efforts to bring about his recovery over the following weeks were in vain. The *Enterprise* noted that Phillip, a carpenter and "man of more than ordinary strength and vigor and a tireless worker," used to visit his son and daughter-in-law during the summers and, for many years, would even work at Perkins.

After Phillip passed away, Lydia moved to Mishawaka and lived in her son's home, where she died on April 10, 1904. Phillip and Lydia Fisher are buried at Bryan's Fountain Grove Cemetery.

Manuel Fisher's term as Mishawaka's chief executive ended after the May 1902 election. Melville Mix, who had been a contender for the Republicans' mayoral nomination in 1899, switched parties and ran as a Democrat against William Miller. Out of 1,782 ballots cast, Mix's margin of victory was 102 votes. Republicans won the clerk, marshal and treasurer races, and the city council was evenly split between the two parties.

The last regular meeting of the old city council occurred on May 5. The *Enterprise* noted "a pleasant relationship between the members during the past three years." Mayor Fisher expressed a similar sentiment regarding his interaction with the councilmen and thanked them "for their aid and good will."

A week later, the changing of the guard took place on the city council. Fisher opened the meeting with all the old members in their usual seats, and in the rear of the chamber, the councilmen-elect waited to take their new posts. Mayor Fisher reviewed the body's accomplishments over the preceding three years and congratulated the members. Echoing the hopes he expressed upon taking office three years earlier, Fisher continued with these words of pride and appreciation for the bipartisan spirit with which the council had acted for the city's welfare:

> *We have labored earnestly for the interests of all citizens; all committees have performed their work and that work was well done. Years hence residents of Mishawaka will recognize the results of the efforts of the first common council of this city. This body can point with pride to that which has been accomplished; it has done its work fearlessly, unflinchingly. I have no apologies to make, for we have transacted municipal business as if it were our own. The question is "Are we satisfied?" As mayor, I have tried to treat all of you cordially; you have trusted me and cooperated with me, both Democrats and Republicans. After assuming our private paths in life, we can allow our minds to grow retrospective and, in reviewing the past, can be proud of it.*

Mayor Fisher concluded by thanking each member of the first city council "for his consideration toward me, his fidelity to his office, and his record as a member of this body."

According to the *Enterprise*, Fisher's remarks "made a deep impression upon those to whom they were addressed," leaving the room in silence until a motion was made to adjourn, "and Mishawaka's first municipal legislative body passed out of existence."

The city clerk then read the names of the councilmen-elect, and Mayor Fisher administered the oath of office to each. Fisher, whose tenure would continue until Mayor-elect Mix took office in September, acknowledged that he and the evenly split new council might have their conflicts but that he would be fair and impartial in breaking any tie votes.

As the old council ended, Ed Jernegan offered his favorable review of their achievements: "Three years ago, Mishawaka was an overgrown town with crude and inadequate local government....What has been accomplished can be readily seen. The improvements made in Mishawaka during the past three years are remarkable. That these additions and improvements have cost considerable is true, but the city has something substantial to show for it and Mishawaka is a city to be proud of, with first-class systems of sewerage and municipal water works and electric lighting service."

The *Tribune* offered similar praise for the "spirit of progress that has marked the city under the careful guidance of Mr. Fisher....Under him Mishawaka has made splendid progress and today occupies a higher position in every way than ever before. Mr. Fisher retires with the satisfaction of knowing that he is credited with having made a most excellent official."

Jernegan was aware of how difficult the jobs of the mayor and council members had been. "Most of the councilmen and city officers, including Mayor Fisher and Clerk Eggleston, are more than glad their terms of service are so nearly ended," he had written in April 1902. "The position of a city official in a growing place like Mishawaka is one of considerable labor, paltry compensation, and plenty of fault-finding and abuse."

On August 25, the city council held a special meeting to address the question of acquiring the right-of-way for approaches to the Cedar Street Bridge, which the St. Joseph County commissioners had proposed to build. In the final legislative action of Fisher's administration, the council approved a resolution to obtain the land needed for the bridge project.

At the following week's regular meeting on September 2, Mayor Fisher called the council to order one last time. The *Enterprise* reported that he "made a brief but feeling speech upon his final relinquishment of the gavel." Fisher thanked both the former and new council for its "assistance in the trying duties of the office which he had faithfully tried to perform," introduced Mayor Mix and "retired to the rear of the room."

Manuel was only out of office for a month when he suffered an unexpected tragedy. After hosting some friends on the evening of October 1, the Fishers had gone to bed. Manuel was awakened at 10:45 p.m. by the sound of Elizabeth choking or gasping. Thinking that she might be dreaming, Manuel shook her shoulder to rouse her, but she did not respond. Turning on the light, he was "horrified" to discover that Libbie was "limp and lifeless," the *Enterprise* reported. Two doctors were called, but they were unable to revive her.

The news of Elizabeth Fisher's death from an apparent heart attack shocked Mishawakans, especially because the fifty-two-year-old had been in excellent health. "Seldom if ever has this community been so sadly stunned as by the startling information" of Libbie's passing, wrote the *Enterprise*. "Her sad and unexpected taking is a crushing blow to a sorrowing circle of friends" and to her "heartbroken husband."

Elizabeth was buried next to her and Manuel's daughter and her parents at South Bend.

Manuel grieved and healed as much as possible. Now a private citizen, he was still president of Perkins Wind Mill Company and remained in his home on East Second Street.

In April 1903, Fisher and twenty-four other leading citizens formed the Mishawaka Public Utilities Company, which took over the municipal waterworks and electric plant and leased them back to the city. This arrangement enabled the extension of water and electric services and payment of bonds. It also helped Mishawaka to build a new city hall, which opened in October 1904.

On December 29, 1903, Manuel surprised his friends and neighbors in Mishawaka by remarrying. Sallie Miller, a native of Clinton County, Ohio, had resided in Mishawaka some twenty years before with her mother, Mary; sister, Anna; and uncle, Dr. R.T. Van Pelt. Sallie, age fifty-five, was a housekeeper in Washington Court House, Ohio, sixty-five miles northeast of Cincinnati, at the time she and Manuel married.

The 1906 city directory lists Fisher as Perkins's president, but the 1908 directory refers to his profession as "cashier North Side Trust & Savings Company." This institution opened in 1907 and was located at the northeast corner of North Bridge (Main) Street and Joseph Street (Mishawaka Avenue). Similar listings for Manuel appear in the 1910, 1912 and 1914 city directories. By the time of the 1916 book, though, he was "retired."

Even at age seventy, Fisher continued his involvement in fraternal organizations and his service as an elder of the First Presbyterian Church. When the Orra L. Snyder Garrison of the Army and Navy Union was formed after World War I, Manuel was its first charter member.

Manuel Fisher died in his home on the evening of April 25, 1919. The *Tribune* reported that the cause of death was "an illness of heart trouble," and

Manuel Fisher, his daughter and his first and second wives are buried at City Cemetery, South Bend. *Author's collection.*

the *Enterprise* noted that Fisher "had been in failing health for a number of years." Three days later, the funeral service was held in the Fisher home, officiated by Reverend Dr. John Burnett of the First Presbyterian Church. Manuel was laid to rest beside Libbie at South Bend City Cemetery. The GAR's Houghton Post conducted the graveside service for its fallen former commander.

Just two and a half months after Manuel passed, Sallie followed him. She also died at home on July 9 after suffering from an illness for five weeks. Sallie was buried next to Manuel, who rests forever between the two women who were his wife.

The Fishers' home at 222 Lincolnway East was sold and continued as a residence. This address last appears in the 1925 city directory, which suggests that the house was demolished and the land sat vacant. By the time of the 1932 city directory, Gafill Oil Company had built a gas station on the property. That structure still stands and is now an Edward Jones Investments office.

When it comes to listing past mayors, Mishawaka citizens are more likely to remember Margaret Prickett and Robert Beutter than they are Manuel Fisher. Nonetheless, Fisher has not been entirely forgotten by the community that was his home for nearly fifty years. Fisher Court (originally Fisher Lane), which opened in 1907, bears his name and runs for just half a block south of Fourth Street near the Princess City Parkway underpass. Manuel's photo hangs in city hall with those of other Mishawaka mayors, and the Heritage Center of the Mishawaka-Penn-Harris Public Library displays a frame with photos of Mayor Fisher and members of the first city council.

In 1838, Henry Wadsworth Longfellow wrote "A Psalm of Life," one of the most popular poems of the nineteenth century. It includes the following lines:

> *Lives of great men all remind us*
> *We can make our lives sublime,*
> *And, departing, leave behind us*
> *Footprints on the sands of time.*

Longfellow's words apply perfectly to Manuel Fisher: Civil War soldier, husband and father, president of Perkins Wind Mill Company, church elder and mayor. By any account, Fisher was a great man in whose footprints the mayors—and citizens—of Mishawaka have walked for more than a century.

Chapter 2

A Rousing Reception

Vice President Fairbanks Visits Mishawaka

O n May 21, 2017, Vice President Mike Pence was the featured speaker at the University of Notre Dame's 172nd Commencement. Pence's visit to St. Joseph County and his words to the graduating class made national headlines, primarily because the news media focused its attention and praise on the hundred or so graduates who disrupted the event by walking out in protest of perceived offenses by President Donald Trump and the vice president. Lost in the media coverage, though, was a significant moment in Mishawaka history. When Pence spent the night of May 20–21 at the Holiday Inn on East Douglas Road, he was likely the first sitting vice president to visit a location within the city limits of Mishawaka since Charles Fairbanks, another Hoosier, in 1908. Fairbanks's brief time in Mishawaka was the most excitement the town had seen since the Great Mishawaka Fire of 1872, yet it appears in no Mishawaka history book and has been mostly forgotten.

Charles Warren Fairbanks is best known today for the city in Alaska named in his honor, but he was one of the major national figures of his day. Born in 1852, Fairbanks was a native Ohioan who came to Indianapolis at age twenty-two and became an attorney with the Chesapeake & Ohio Railroad. Fairbanks rose to prominence in the state's Republican Party, and his campaign work in 1892 led to a close friendship with Ohio governor William McKinley. As the leader of the Republican Party in Indiana and majority owner of the *Indianapolis News*, Fairbanks delivered Indiana for McKinley in the 1896 presidential election. He also helped build Republican

Vice President Charles W. Fairbanks. *Mishawaka Historical Museum.*

majorities in the state legislature, which appointed Fairbanks to the U.S. Senate in 1897. Fairbanks was appointed to the Joint High Commission that decided the U.S.-Canada border in Alaska, and he earned the gratitude of Alaskans by asserting his opposition to "the yielding of an inch of United States territory." In an effort to balance their 1904 ticket ideologically and geographically, the Republicans chose Charles Fairbanks as their vice presidential candidate, and he was elected the twenty-sixth vice president of the United States. President Theodore Roosevelt refused to give Fairbanks any substantial role in the administration, so the Hoosier was limited to his constitutionally defined duty of presiding over the Senate, where he often worked against Roosevelt's Square Deal. When Roosevelt did not run for reelection in 1908, Fairbanks sought the Republican nomination but lost to William Howard Taft. Ever the loyal soldier, Fairbanks nonetheless campaigned for his party's candidates, especially the ticket of Taft and James Sherman, who were running against William Jennings Bryan, the Democratic nominee, and his vice presidential pick, John Kern of Indiana. It is in this capacity that Vice President Fairbanks came to Mishawaka one evening in late October 1908.

Fairbanks's visit was the highlight of two weeks of frenzied political activity in Mishawaka preceding the November 3 general election. On Tuesday, October 20, Leslie Shaw, a former governor of Iowa and secretary of the treasury from 1902 to 1907, spoke to a capacity crowd at the Century Theater, also known as the "opera house," in the Phoenix Building on the 100 block of West Second Street. According to the Republican *Mishawaka Enterprise*, Shaw received frequent applause "during his witty, logical, and forceful presentation on sound Republican doctrines" and was given warm personal greetings by many afterward.

The next evening, Charles Miller, the local Republican candidate for Congress, spoke at the Century Theater. Again, a large audience was on hand. The *Enterprise* offered another favorable review of the rally: "Mr. Miller was in fine form and made a stirring speech which elicited frequent and hearty applause and created an excellent impression."

On Friday, October 23, Democrats turned out in huge numbers to hear Henry Barnhart, their party's nominee for Congress. According to the *South Bend Daily Times*, a Democratic newspaper, a standing room–only gathering of more than one thousand people filled the Century Theater to give Barnhart "a royal welcome." Before the event, downtown Mishawaka became a giant political rally. "Hundreds of men in line, bright lights burning, scores cheering, the city band playing popular airs, crowds lining the curb on the north and on the south sides in spite of the drizzling rain," the *Daily Times* described.

The same issue of the *Enterprise* that reported on the Shaw and Miller campaign appearances also made the big announcement that Vice President Fairbanks would be speaking in Mishawaka on Wednesday, October 28. The notice included a picture of the vice president and a brief paragraph that told Mishawakans, "Turn out and hear the distinguished orator."

The *South Bend Tribune*, another Republican newspaper, previewed the Fairbanks visit in its October 27 issue, including details of the parade through downtown that would precede the vice president's speech.

Prominent Republican candidates and campaigners were eager to woo Mishawaka voters, it seemed. The *Daily Times* noted this phenomenon with sarcastic amazement: "It would almost appear that Mishawaka had become [the] pivotal peg around which [the] entire political disc revolves, especially so far as the Republican half of the plate is concerned....It would appear that this city's decision on Nov. 3 will turn the entire tide of the nation."

Campaign events in Mishawaka were happening almost daily during the final week before the election. The *Tribune* article that publicized Fairbanks's visit also summarized "a regular old-time Republican love feast" that was held in the Century Theater on Monday evening, October 26. Nearly every Republican candidate for county and township offices was on stage, and each spoke briefly to the large crowd, asking for support.

James Watson, the Republican candidate for governor, came to Mishawaka the following day and made two appearances. At noon, he spoke to five hundred employees at the Mishawaka Woolen Company and, in the *Tribune*'s judgment, "left a most favorable impression." After traveling to Notre Dame and South Bend, Watson returned to Mishawaka for a 4:00 p.m. address at the Century Theater. Despite the unusual time for such an event, the theater "was filled with voters and ladies." According to the *Tribune* account, Watson "delivered the most earnest, enthusing, and convincing speech delivered during the campaign in this city. He was frequently interrupted by applause." The *Enterprise*, whose editor was master of ceremonies at the event, naturally concurred, stating that Watson's speech was "a masterly presentation of campaign issues and sound Republican policies and created great enthusiasm among his hearers."

The *Daily Times* was decidedly less impressed by Watson's appearance. Its article began with reference to a "fair-sized audience" and reported that Watson had been half an hour late for the rally. It also noted that the Republican candidate admitted that his party had not "cleaned out the trusts but that it is doing a great thing in trying."

On October 28, the day of Fairbanks's visit to Mishawaka, the *Tribune* again advertised the event in hopes of encouraging a large crowd for the vice president:

> *Vice-President in Mishawaka Tonight*
> *Vice-President Charles W. Fairbanks Will Speak in the Century Theater in Misha-Waka This Evening at Eight O'clock. Mishawaka Citizens Are Preparing to Give Him a Rousing Reception. They De-Sire to Have the People of South Bend Participate.*

Before coming to Mishawaka, Vice President Fairbanks arrived in Elkhart at the Big Four railroad depot. Known more formally as the Cleveland, Cincinnati, Chicago & St. Louis Railway, the Big Four was a separate railroad from the Lake Shore & Michigan Southern, which also went through Elkhart and connected Mishawaka and South Bend with Chicago and New York City.

Vice President Fairbanks and his private secretary, George Lockwood, arrived at the Big Four station at 4:00 p.m. They were met by a contingent of nine Mishawakans, including Mayor Charles Frank, former mayor Manuel Fisher, James Roper of the Roper Furniture Company, *Mishawaka Enterprise* editor and owner Edward Jernegan, businessmen Frederick Eberhart Jr. and Francis Eberhart, Reverend Alfred Ormond, Reverend LeRoy Bobbitt and Reverend C. Claude Travis. These representatives then escorted Fairbanks and Lockwood the twelve miles to Mishawaka in a small caravan of automobiles.

Before reaching downtown, the local leaders brought the vice president to St. Paul's Episcopal Church at the northeast corner of East Second Street (Lincolnway) and Cedar Street, arriving there after 5:00 p.m. Fairbanks was the guest of honor at the annual Bishop Knickerbacker Guild supper, held in the church's basement, or undercroft. Bishop David Buel Knickerbacker, the fourth bishop of the Episcopal Diocese of Indiana, had died suddenly of

St. Paul's Episcopal Church shortly after the building was completed in 1907. *Mishawaka-Penn-Harris Public Library.*

an illness in 1894, and the Mishawaka congregation had named its sodality in memory of the popular clergyman.

According to the *Enterprise*'s account, "Mr. Fairbanks's entry was greeted with hearty applause by the throng of patrons at the supper." The *South Bend News* reported that three hundred persons were in attendance, which means that the small space was jam-packed with people eager to share a meal with the nation's second-highest official. The room was decorated with patriotic colors and posters of political candidates. The women of the guild prepared the meal, and it was served by the men of the church. The vice president, the prominent citizens who met him in Elkhart, and other members of the larger official reception committee were seated at special tables.

"The supper was a great success," wrote the *Tribune*, "and the guest of honor heartily enjoyed the hospitality." Vice President Fairbanks was asked to give a short after-dinner speech, during which he thanked the women of the Knickerbacker Guild for their courtesy. Fairbanks also praised the event's spirit of community and noted favorably that clergy from several denominations had come together for the supper. He added that he thought highly of the work done by churches and believed, in the *Tribune*'s words, "good politics came with Christianity."

When the dinner concluded, Vice President Fairbanks went to the adjacent rectory, where he shook hands and greeted as many people as he could. At about 7:00 p.m., Fairbanks, Mayor Frank and the reception committee left St. Paul's and traveled by car to the Frank residence at 813 West Second Street. A thousand people had already filled the street in front of the home, eagerly anticipating the vice president's arrival and the ensuing political parade through downtown. Not since South Bend's Schuyler Colfax was vice president in the Ulysses S. Grant administration thirty-five years earlier had a sitting U.S. vice president visited Mishawaka, and never had any political figure brought out thousands of residents onto the city's streets. Fairbanks felt compelled to briefly address the crowd from the Franks' front porch, and Mayor Frank also offered a few remarks. Vice President Fairbanks, his hosts and the committee relaxed inside for a short while before the procession began.

"At 7:30 the streets of Mishawaka were crowded with people from Spring to Main Streets and from Second Street to Joseph Street [Mishawaka Avenue] on the north side of the river, and it seemed as if all Mishawaka had turned out to do honor to this great statesman," the *Tribune* described.

The parade formed at the intersection of Smith Street and Second Street, two doors west of the Frank house. The lineup was led by a marching band, followed by seventy horsemen and ten touring cars that included Fairbanks and the reception committee. Two companies of the Presbyterian Cadets of America, boys in full uniform, acted as an honor guard for the vice president. The procession continued with another band, a group of two hundred Republicans, ward club organizations, the Young Voters' Drum Corps, the Eberhart Drum Corps and finally hundreds of other Republican faithful marching to spirited musical numbers. The *Tribune* reported, "The procession was over a mile in length, and over 2,000 men were on horseback, in automobiles, and on foot."

The darkness of a late October evening had already fallen over Mishawaka, but "the parade was brilliantly lighted with red fire and fireworks by the marchers," the *Enterprise* explained. Three blocks into the line of march— between Towle Avenue and West Street—a wagonload of rockets, Roman candles and other pyrotechnics caught fire. Eight men jumped off the wagon, and the frightened horses were unhitched. The *Daily Times* reported that the mishap caused the crowd to scurry away from a possible explosion, but no injuries resulted—only minor damage to the wagon and a few burned fireworks.

Vice President Fairbanks campaigning in Menominee, Michigan, on September 10, 1908. His appearance in downtown Mishawaka would have resembled this scene. *Mishawaka Historical Museum.*

The massive parade, referred to by the *Tribune* as "a monster demonstration," continued east on Second to Main, north and across the river to Joseph and then "counter marched" back to the intersection of Main and Second. At the Four Corners, an estimated five to six thousand people waited excitedly for the vice president to arrive for his speech at the Century Theater. The turnout was impressive, especially given that Mishawaka had a population of approximately 10,500 in 1908.

With thousands of excited people lining downtown streets and an enormous throng packed into the intersection of Main and Second, an errant fireworks wagon was not the only mayhem on Mishawaka's streets that evening. Abraham DeBaun found himself in the path of an oncoming streetcar and was saved by William Zweigle, the parade marshal, who pushed DeBaun away just before he would have been run over. The *Enterprise* also reported that pickpockets were at work in the crowd, victimizing at least three people for amounts ranging from a few dollars to ten dollars. Revealing its true political colors, the *Daily Times* devoted five paragraphs to the pickpockets, adding with feigned concern, "It is horrifying to contemplate that Vice President Fairbanks would bring with him a lot of rascals who would dare rob our Republican residents of their money."

Long before Fairbanks arrived, the Century Theater had been filled to capacity with perhaps another thousand Republican supporters, and many more had been turned away. To avoid upsetting any potential voter, the vice president decided to address the crowd outside from the back of his automobile, which had stopped in front of the Milburn House, Mishawaka's finest hotel, on the east side of Main Street. After Mayor Frank introduced him, Fairbanks spoke to the cheering assemblage for fifteen to twenty minutes, but the large and enthusiastic crowd made it difficult to understand what he was saying. Meanwhile, a singing quartet entertained the crowd in the theater until Fairbanks came inside.

When the vice president finally walked on stage, followed by the reception committee and other special guests, "he was given cheer after cheer and the ovation lasted for several minutes," the *Tribune* reported in its account. Along with those seated or standing in the packed house, a hundred people shared the stage with Fairbanks.

After another song by the quartet, Mayor Frank introduced Vice President Fairbanks, according to the *Tribune*, "as Indiana's most distinguished citizen and one whom the nation delights to honor."

This photo of Main and Second Streets shows the Phoenix Building, *right*, and the Milburn House beyond it. *Mishawaka-Penn-Harris Public Library.*

Fairbanks spoke to the convocation of Republican enthusiasts for more than an hour. He began by expressing pleasure at the "prosperity and marvelous growth" of Mishawaka he had noticed since his last visit in 1894. The vice president referred to a recent visit to South Bend, where he had dedicated the new YMCA building: "When I was at South Bend last Sunday, I heard an address by a speaker in which he said that if Mishawaka were incorporated in South Bend the plan would be beneficial to both cities. When I came to this city, they said that it was South Bend that should be incorporated into Mishawaka." The remark brought an appreciative cheer from the audience.

After complimenting Mishawaka, Fairbanks moved on to the substance of his talk, which was an explanation of Republican beliefs and endorsement of GOP candidates in the upcoming election. He said he would not speak negatively of the Democratic candidates or their political philosophy. The vice president even stated it was good that Americans have differing politics because no party was without flaw and discussing these differences would lead to truths that benefited the nation. "The great question," he stated, "is which party is nearly right."

Fairbanks then reminded his listeners that there was not just an important national election to be decided in November. "The state ticket, in my judgment, is as important as the national," he asserted. The speaker praised the qualifications of Republican gubernatorial nominee James Watson and congressional candidate Charles Miller and urged voters to do all they could to see the men were elected.

Fairbanks also touted his party's accomplishments since the Civil War and attacked the Democrats for their failed, inconsistent policies: "The Republican Party has a record of 40 years—it is a record of achievements. On the other hand, the Democratic Party can not show a great act that it has on record for that time since 1861 worthy to be called a record of fulfillment....For what has that party done since 1861?"

The vice president paused his partisanship in order to encourage the audience to do their civic duty by voting. "'What is the value of my vote among millions?' is too frequently asked," Fairbanks complained. "This is a very unpatriotic view. Vote some ticket, the one you think is right, and enjoy the suffrage which cost our forefathers toil and blood. Approach the booth with a patriotic spirit and cast a ballot. Do not vote a Republican ticket or a Democratic ticket simply because your ancestor did, but do credit to them by casting for the right issues, and to the best of your judgment."

Fairbanks drew from recent political history to make his case for the Republicans. During the presidency of Benjamin Harrison, 1889–93, the nation was prosperous, he said, yet the Democrats ousted Harrison in favor of Grover Cleveland and passed the low Wilson-Gorman Tariff Act, resulting in the worst financial panic of the nineteenth century. When Fairbanks went overseas to assess the economic situation and to study tariff policy, he found a factory in Manchester, England, making woolens for export to the United States while at the same time American manufacturers were shutting down and millions were unemployed.

"The Wilson bill stopped work here but made the factories of other countries busy," the speaker asserted. "It served to paralyze the industrial system of the United States and made work in England; closed doors of opportunity here and opened factories elsewhere. I came back determined to work with all my ability to kill such a policy, for the Wilson bill was not American in spirit." Fairbanks reminded the Mishawakans that, as their senator, he had helped replace the Wilson-Gorman Tariff Act with the protectionist Dingley Act. After McKinley won the presidency in 1896, the Republicans' gold standard and high tariffs kept the country prosperous for a decade and benefited workers, the vice president noted, but currency proposals in the Democratic platform would lead to inflation and stagnant economic growth.

Fairbanks admitted that there had been an economic downturn in 1907, but "in comparison with the Democratic panic, it was like a May zephyr to a Kansas cyclone. They were as unlike as day is from night." He blamed "ten years of remarkable prosperity and extravagance" for the previous year's panic, rather than Republican tariff and gold policies. The vice president admitted that high tariffs were not "panic-proof" and would not always mean full employment. He felt the issue voters must consider is which party and its policies would best promote prosperity over the long term:

> *In the effort to regain a full measure of good times, would you overturn those who have always brought prosperity and repeat the error of several years ago? The Republican and Democratic parties are not equally suited to operate a government. It wants a party with sound principles. Was the Democratic Party sound in 1906? No and it is not today....We want a government which will induce the mills to run the greater share of the time and employ most of the people the greatest number of days in the year. You cannot get these conditions under free trade or tariff for revenue only. Are we going to trust this matter to chance, or are we going to decide this question by the ballot box?*

Fairbanks closed his remarks with one last appeal on behalf of Republican candidates: "In a few days, you will render your decision and see to it that you elect James E. Watson for governor of Indiana, Hon. C.W. Miller for congressman of this district, and William Howard Taft President of the United States."

After the address in the Century Theater, "hundreds of people shook hands with" Vice President Fairbanks, the *Tribune* reported. He then traveled to South Bend by automobile, followed by many members of the Mishawaka reception committee in other cars. The vice president spent the night in South Bend and departed for LaGrange the next day.

Local newspapers described Fairbanks's crowded hours in Mishawaka through politically tinted lenses. In its coverage on October 29, the *South Bend Tribune* gushed enthusiastically about the success of Fairbanks's visit. Under the headline "Great Ovation to Fairbanks" and subheadline "Parade Grand Success," its coverage began by stating that Fairbanks "received an ovation in Mishawaka…never before accorded to any man of the nation in the history of this city." The article also noted that the vice president's "great popularity…was seen in the welcome and demonstration accorded him" in Mishawaka and that Fairbanks "acknowledged that it was the largest demonstration he had seen in the entire country in a city the size of Mishawaka."

In its next issue two days after Fairbanks's visit, the *Mishawaka Enterprise* expressed similar glowing sentiments. With the headline of "A Rousing Rally," its article referred to the reception as "a crowning credit to Mishawaka and Penn Township and a pleasing tribute to the personality and prominence of Mr. Fairbanks." The paper also complimented the city's Republican leadership for "bringing about the marked success of the great rally."

The *South Bend News* reported on the Fairbanks visit in more objective terms, emphasizing the size of the event, offering several paragraphs of the vice president's quoted remarks and describing the supper at St. Paul's Church.

The *South Bend Daily Times*, though, could not hide its annoyance about what Mishawaka Republicans had pulled off. Its headline was "High Officer Here," the subheadlines referred to the "privilege" of hosting the vice president and the "great ovation" that Fairbanks received and the "entertainment" was described as "royal" and the "demonstration brilliant." A few paragraphs later, though, the *Daily Times*' article opined that Republicans had been "jealous" after the huge Democratic rally for Barnhart the previous Friday and "pressed into service every available man" in order to surpass their rivals' show of enthusiasm. The *Daily Times* also stated that the horsemen and many of the marchers had "been drafted" into the parade and the Presbyterian cadets "were pulled into line," suggesting that they participated only reluctantly or even against their will. The paper also turned its coverage into an editorial by stating that Fairbanks offered no specific plans against currency inflation and that the Republican Party "has so long been in power and accomplished little in the direction referred to." The *Daily Times* accused Mishawaka police of having a double standard favoring Republican rallies. When people inside the theater complained that the crowd outside was so loud that they could not hear Fairbanks, Police Chief Benjamin Jarrett and his men "made everybody be good, ordering ladies and men and girls to 'cut out!' the blowing of tin horns." The *Daily Times* noted that such efforts were absent during the Barnhart rally. Its article also observed that Republicans had been allowed to schedule speeches and demonstrations during Democratic events, but no such "counter attractions" were allowed "when the Republicans do their great stunt."

Mishawaka had not even two full days to rest and recover from the excitement of Vice President Fairbanks's visit before the final political celebrity of the season came to town. The Thursday, October 29 *Tribune* announced that Indiana's senior U.S. senator, Albert Beveridge, would make a brief stop at the Lake Shore depot around 4:50 p.m. the next day. A large crowd gathered at the intersection of South Main and the Lake Shore tracks to hear the popular Beveridge speak. Although it was cold and windy and the senator's special train was forty minutes late, the *Tribune* estimated that at least a thousand supporters braved the elements and stayed until Beveridge arrived.

Four days later, Mishawakans and their countrymen went to the polls. Interest in the election's outcome was so great that two thousand people congregated downtown to watch as results were projected by stereopticon from the Dodge Club at the northeast corner of Main and Second onto a giant screen hung on the side of the Guaranty Building, which stood on the northwest corner of the intersection. Others read the vote totals in the windows of the Red Cross Pharmacy at 104 West Second or the Robinson & McFarland Drug Store at 101 East Second, and some visited the *Tribune*'s Mishawaka office at 119 South Main, where local tallies were delivered by messengers and national results came by telephone. In the Century Theater, both the Democratic and Republican central committees waited anxiously for election updates with many of their faithful.

Inspired by Vice President Fairbanks's appearance, Mishawakans voted overwhelmingly Republican and helped elect William Howard Taft the next president of the United States. Fairbanks's message that William Jennings Bryan and the Democrats would harm American industry with low tariffs and inflated currency resonated in a town filled with factory workers. Taft defeated Bryan in each of Mishawaka's wards and precincts, often by overwhelming margins. Only in the heavily Democratic 3rd Ward were the totals even close. James Watson, the Republican candidate for governor, also dominated the Mishawaka vote, but Democrat Thomas Marshall did manage to win three precincts. In the statewide election, Marshall eked out a narrow victory, 48.1 percent to 48 percent, enabling the Democrats to reclaim the governor's office for the first time since 1897. In the 13th District Congressional race, Henry Barnhart defeated Charles Miller, but the local newspapers did not report how Mishawaka precincts voted in this contest. Despite Marshall and Barnhart's wins, Republicans, who won several key races in Penn Township and St. Joseph County, were "joyous" and celebrating a "remarkable victory," according to the next day's *Tribune*.

Charles Fairbanks finished out the remaining four months of his vice presidency and came back to Indiana. His political career was not over, though. After the Republican Party divided over Theodore Roosevelt's Bull Moose candidacy in 1912, Fairbanks urged party unity. He made an unsuccessful bid for the Republican nomination in 1916 and instead reluctantly agreed to be Charles Evans Hughes's running mate. The Hughes-Fairbanks ticket narrowly lost to Woodrow Wilson and another Hoosier vice president, Thomas Marshall. After his last campaign, Charles Fairbanks returned to his law practice in Indianapolis, where he died on June 4, 1918. He is buried at Crown Hill Cemetery, Indianapolis.

After the excitement of October 28, 1908, Charles Fairbanks never again returned to Mishawaka. Not until sixty years later would another national political figure bring thousands of cheering Mishawakans onto the streets of downtown. When Democratic presidential candidate Senator Robert Kennedy spoke to a huge crowd at the corner of Main and Lincolnway on May 2, 1968, he stood on a platform near the First National Bank, almost exactly where Vice President Fairbanks gave his impromptu speech outside the Milburn House. One wonders how many people attended *both* the Fairbanks and Kennedy appearances.

The buildings that briefly hosted Vice President Fairbanks during his visit to Mishawaka so long ago have met varied fates. The Century Theater continued as a venue for motion pictures, vaudeville and other live productions until it closed in the mid-1920s. That half of the Phoenix Building was demolished in 1937 and replaced by a single-story F.W. Woolworth's five-and-dime store,

The Century Theater, where Vice President Fairbanks spoke, was located in the west half of the Phoenix Building, which has since been demolished. *Mishawaka-Penn-Harris Public Library.*

which stayed in business until 1976 or 1977. The Indiana Fencing Academy has occupied the building since 1992. A generation of fencers learned to lunge and parry in the same space where Charles Fairbanks once made jabs at William Jennings Bryan and the Democrats.

Charles Frank served as mayor until 1910 and died the following year at age sixty-eight, one of the most esteemed men in town. According to city directories, his house at 813 Lincoln Way West stood until 1958 or 1959. That site today is a parking lot for Salon Bella Mia, whose customers have no idea that their vehicles sit near the spot where the Vice President of the United States spoke to a thousand enthusiastic supporters before parading through the streets of Mishawaka.

Only St. Paul's Episcopal Church survives to bear witness to Fairbanks's campaign appearance. Much has changed in Mishawaka since 1908, but Vice President Fairbanks would still recognize St. Paul's, where he was the guest of honor at the Bishop Knickerbacker Guild supper. Although it has probably not seen a crowd of three hundred people since Fairbanks's visit, the undercroft remains an attractive space where much fellowship and countless parish events have taken place over the years. It also evokes the 113-year-old memory of a few thrilling hours in the political life of Mishawaka.

CHAPTER 3

ONE GLORIOUS DAY

Mishawaka's Independence Day Celebration of 1909

For the past several years, South Bend has designated the first week of June as "Best Week Ever," holding events throughout the city to celebrate "creativity, culture, and progress as a community." While the title's hyperbole may be new, the concept of scheduling together many exciting activities to promote tourism, business and civic pride has been around for a long time. On July 5, 1909, Mishawaka's business and municipal leaders hosted a Historical Pageant and Fourth of July Celebration that still ranks as the most exciting day in the city's history.

The impetus for staging a daylong celebration came from the construction of the Hotel Mishawaka at the southeast corner of Main and Third Streets. In order to create a modern hotel in the city center, the Mishawaka Business Men's Association purchased the land on which the hotel would be built, and the Mishawaka Public Improvement Corporation carried out its construction in 1908 and 1909. The corporation's leaders were a who's who of Mishawaka business and politics: former mayor Melville Mix, head of the Dodge Manufacturing Company, was president; Frederick Eberhart, superintendent of the Mishawaka Woolen Manufacturing Company, was vice president; and Mayor Charles Frank was treasurer.

The hotel cost $125,000 to build and immediately became one of the downtown's signature structures. Built in Spanish Mission style, the four-story edifice featured corner towers, a red tile roof, an elaborate white mortar entrance from Main Street and a veranda facing Third and Main Streets. Inside, the elegant hotel included sixty-five guest rooms and a beautifully decorated lobby.

The Hotel Mishawaka under construction. *Mishawaka Historical Museum.*

Work on the hotel was nearing completion in the spring of 1909, and city leaders sought to have a grand opening worthy of the magnificent landmark. Prompted by a petition drive in April, the Mishawaka Business Men's Association had decided to undertake another substantial downtown improvement: installing an electric streetlight system, which it would donate to the city. Businesses' and individuals' "subscriptions" quickly covered the $20,000 cost of the project. The dedication of both the hotel and the streetlight system soon conflated with the annual Independence Day celebration as plans developed for a day filled with historical pageantry, a massive parade, speeches, bands, athletic contests and fireworks.

Organizers appealed to Mishawakans to attend but also to people in surrounding counties and to former residents who had moved away, thus adding a homecoming element to the festivities. The intent was partly a form of civic evangelization, enticing people to move to Mishawaka in order to increase its population to 25,000 by 1915. Such an objective seemed realistic given that Mishawaka had already grown from 5,560 residents in 1900 to more than 10,000.

At its June 1 meeting, the Mishawaka Business Men's Association formally decided to use Independence Day to dedicate the streetlight system and to open the Hotel Mishawaka. Because July 4 fell on a Sunday, the organization needed to keep the Sabbath holy and avoid conflicts with church services;

The "All for Mishawaka" emblem was featured prominently during the events of July 5, 1909. *Author's collection.*

instead, its full day's program of activities would be held on July 5. The *Mishawaka Enterprise* of June 4 reported on these exciting plans and unveiled the city's new slogan and design, which would be featured at the celebration: a four-leaf clover with the leaves saying "No North Side, No East End, No South Side, No West End." The center said, "25,000 in 1915," and surrounding it were the words "All for Mishawaka." The emblem, created by Kenyon Mix and the Sales Promotion Company, was put on pins and posters that were soon all over town.

During the next month, local newspapers regularly featured articles about the upcoming celebration. North side businessmen did not want to be left in the dark when the new streetlights were installed downtown. At its June 14 meeting, the North Side Boosters Club authorized a committee to extend the streetlight system north of the river. Starting the week of June 21, light posts were installed downtown, and the Mishawaka Business Men's Association voted that day to also place lights north of the river. Their contractor, M.V. Cheesman & Company, expressed confidence that both the north and south commercial districts would shine brilliantly when the switch was flipped on the evening of July 5. The streetlights on North Main were briefly tested on July 1, the remaining glass globes were put in place on July 2, and the north side lights were completed the next day.

The Hotel Mishawaka was also hurrying to put on its finishing touches but was "as yet scarcely ready to accommodate patrons," wrote the *Enterprise* on July 2. The Beiger Furniture Company, which had the contract to furnish the hotel, received the last train carloads of furniture on July 1. The furniture was assembled at the hotel as quickly as wagons could transport it from the freight depot. The *South Bend Tribune* reported on June 29 that a "corps of expert waitresses," an "expert chef" and an "expert pastry cook" were coming from Chicago the next day, and more than one hundred workers were hurrying to finish the dining rooms, kitchen and guest rooms. Guests began arriving on July 2, even though the hotel was neither officially open nor fully furnished.

Preparations for the big day continued in other areas too, including selecting the persons to play the starring roles of Princess Mishawaka and Chief Elkhart. The honor of being the princess was determined by a two-

Mishawaka's new streetlight system is shown here in 1909, looking west on Second Street toward the Phoenix Building. *Mishawaka-Penn-Harris Public Library.*

week voting contest that concluded at midnight on June 30. Two days later, results were announced. Twenty-one-year-old Jennie Skelly garnered 3,802 votes to take first, narrowly ahead of the runner-up's 3,761 tallies. The same *Enterprise* article that announced Miss Skelly's election also stated that Frederick Eberhart, age forty-five, would play Chief Elkhart.

To generate a huge turnout, organizers marketed the celebration throughout the area. Beginning the week of June 28, local street railway companies began sending out "boom cars" loudly advertising the July 5 events. On Saturday, July 3, the Chicago, South Bend & Northern Indiana Railway donated the use of one of its cars to publicize the Mishawaka celebration. Twenty-five "lusty-lunged boomers" with "horns, megaphones and other noise-producing devices," according to the *Enterprise*, came along as the vibrantly bedecked vehicle traveled to South Bend, Michigan City, LaPorte, Goshen and other cities, even as far as Hammond. In addition to interurban advertising, four automobile boom cars were sent out to cities and towns on July 1. The *Enterprise* reported that the autos were "gaudily decorated" with patriotic colors and large signs and even included a bugler on board. Some of the cities and towns visited by the boom cars were South Bend, Niles, St. Joseph, Walkerton, Plymouth, Warsaw, Goshen and Elkhart. On the evening of July 3, a "boom parade" left celebration headquarters in the Phoenix Building to travel throughout South Bend. Anyone who owned a car was invited to decorate it in the municipal colors of green and gold, join the caravan headed west and make lots of noise.

Newspaper advertisements were also used. The *Enterprise*'s ad included the large headlines, "Spend One Glorious Day, July 5th, at Mishawaka, Ind." and "If You've Lived Here, Come Back—If Not, Visit Us." It also touted "Mammoth Special Features and Free Attractions."

Prior to the big day, the streets of Mishawaka were festively decorated. Large cloverleaf emblems with the "All for Mishawaka" motto were placed on buildings at the corner of Main and Second Streets. A committee adorned telephone poles and the two bridges—Cedar and Main—with the national and municipal colors. Strings of Japanese lanterns were hung on the Cedar Street Bridge to lead crowds to Edgewater Drive, where they could best view the fireworks show. Businesses and homeowners were urged to festoon their buildings as an expression of patriotism and community pride. The *Enterprise* of July 2 noted that "immense quantities of bunting, flags and other accessories are being purchased."

Plans for July 5 also included supplying adequate food, water and medical care for tens of thousands of people. Meals would be provided by the Hotel Mishawaka, restaurants, several churches, concession stands and even private homes. A permanent drinking fountain had recently been placed in Battell Park, and several businesses had installed temporary sources of water in front of their establishments. Perkins Wind Mill Company simultaneously provided a community service and advertised its product line by placing two drinking fountains and water tanks on Main Street. As for the crowd's health needs, members of the Physicians' Club agreed to take turns donating their services for an hour in the St. Joseph Field Hospital to be located at the northeast corner of Church and Third Streets. They were assisted by nurses from the Poor Handmaids of Jesus Christ, and two ambulances would be ready for emergencies.

The Mishawaka Police Department had also been preparing for July 5. Several days before the event, patrols were increased, and still more were to be added on the day of the celebration. Twenty-five deputies were sworn in on July 3, and the city jail was cleaned and made ready for any visitors needing incarceration.

It was soon evident that the newspaper articles, advertisements and boom cars were achieving their desired effect. By Saturday afternoon, the railway stations reported that two thousand people had already arrived in Mishawaka.

After weeks of anticipation, Mishawakans awoke with excitement on the morning of July 5, a day that none would ever forget. Day-trippers began coming early, "the steam and electric cars being crowded to their capacity," the *Tribune* stated in its account. Activities commenced at 8:00 a.m. with a "general reception of the city's guests," according to the day's official program. At 8:30 a.m., the interurban singles tennis tournament began at the Penn Tennis Club, located at the northwest corner of Third and Union Streets. Half an hour later, Otto Johnson climbed a ladder atop Ripple Milling Company at the north end of Main Street and dove spectacularly fifty feet into the waters of the south race.

These events were a mere prelude to a historical "star pageant" at 10:00 a.m. featuring dozens of reenactors in Indian attire. As ten thousand people watched silently and respectfully from both sides of the river and from the Cedar Street Bridge, fifty children from St. Joseph School in Indian clothing gathered on the south bank. Two shots were fired, the signal for two Indian scouts in canoes to round the bend beyond Edgewater Drive and continue toward the bridge. The scouts found the area satisfactory, and two more shots were fired. What followed was a remarkable sight as the remainder of the large Indian contingent—dozens of local men, members of the Mishawaka and South Bend chapters of the Order of Red Men, dressed as American Indians—proceeded down the river on canoes.

Waiting to greet this homecoming were city officials, who stood on the river bank between the bridge and St. Paul's Episcopal Church. They included Mayor Frank, City Attorney William O'Neill, members of the Common Council and several prominent businessmen. The first Indian to land was the prophet, played by Carl Chapman, followed by the sachem, senior sagamore, junior sagamore and senior prophet.

Then came the dramatic arrival of Chief Elkhart and Princess Mishawaka. "As Chief Elkhart, with his arm around the princess, came proudly down the river, standing erect in his canoe, the gathering of red men fell on their knees and welcomed him and his daughter home," wrote the *South Bend News*. The chief and princess were formally introduced to the city officials, and Mayor Frank, referred to in the article as "the chief of the pale faces," presented the keys to the city to Chief Elkhart, who gave them to his daughter.

Mayor Frank then requested a prophecy for his city. The prophet faced the sun, raised his hands on high and spoke with a "deep, sonorous" voice:

Oh, great sun that has often kissed the swarthy brows of the warriors and the soft cheeks of the maidens of the forest, behold the upturned cheek and the outstretched palm of your feeble child and may what he utters shed light and hope in the hearts of those who are listening. Give wisdom to my words and turn my eye to the great suns to come, so that I may tell them of the story of happiness and brotherly love that will be theirs and the great destination of their beautiful village of Mishawaka.

Oh, pale face brothers, the Great Spirit created all men equal. He has placed you in his greatest valley beside his most beautiful stream. The smile of the sun lights up your face by the day, and the moon sheds her soft blessings upon you at night, and here you shall live and be happy in freedom, friendship, charity, and brotherly love.

The Great Spirit sees you harnessing the waters of your swift river and sees you teaching it to toil for the children of men. Here shall be the greatest of villages in this valley, whose ceaseless song is one of busy industry and good will. Here you will build great wigwams, and in all material things shall you prosper. Your fame shall spread wherever the sun shines, and you will be called blessed among the blessed.

Finally, when the suns have passed into the great suns and hundreds of great suns have gone by, then those who shall abound and flourish here will speak your name in honor, love, and reverence for the labor you have wrought to prepare for them the great and beautiful village in which they shall live.

A mix of imagined American Indian theology, civic boosterism and idealism, the prophet's words reveal how Mishawakans wanted to see themselves and their city's future advancement.

After the prophecy, the Indian delegation and city officials walked through two archways decorated in patriotic colors to Second Street, where Chief Elkhart, Princess Mishawaka and the Indian children boarded floats. The sixty accompanying warriors mounted horses, and led by a band, all proceeded to the intersection of Main and Second, where they joined in the massive parade that was about to wind its way through Mishawaka.

What the crowd had witnessed along the riverbank that morning was extraordinary, the likes of which had not occurred in nearly a century and will never be seen again. "The river pageant…was something unique in its conception and strikingly beautiful and effective in its presentation," asserted the *Enterprise*.

Even the South Bend newspapers, sometimes reluctant to give favorable attention to Mishawaka, were impressed. The *Tribune* stated, "The pageant, which was without doubt the feature of the day, was declared by all to be one of the most beautiful spectacles of the kind ever presented." The *News* described the Indian homecoming as "picturesque," "carried out with pomp and splendor" and acted with "impressive solemnity."

After the Indian homecoming, attention turned to what the *Tribune* called a "grand industrial pageant," a massive parade consisting of 106 floats, seven bands and a bugle corps. To offer perspective on the size of the 1909 celebration, the June 25 issue of the *Enterprise* had noted that previously the city's largest Independence Day parade, held in 1901, had included fewer than half this number of entries.

The two-mile line of march began with formation on West Street and then proceeded on West Second Street (Lincolnway) to Main, north to Grove Street, east to Division Street, south to Joseph Street (Mishawaka Avenue), east to Cedar Street, south to Second, west to Main and south to Fourth Street. The parade began at 10:30 a.m.

Organized into five divisions, each led by a band, the parade entries represented nearly every civic group and business in town. Because few automobiles or trucks were available, floats were necessarily horse-drawn wagons, making the parade also the largest equine gathering in the city's history. Newspaper accounts refer to one float being pulled by six horses.

The parade wound its way through the streets of Mishawaka. Here, Dodge Manufacturing floats pass celebration headquarters and turn from West Second Street onto North Main Street. *Mishawaka-Penn-Harris Public Library.*

The Allen Hosterman entry, though, found another form of motive power: a team of boys in harnesses.

William Miller was parade marshal and led the first division, which included the Mishawaka police force and the LaPorte City Band. The line of march halted at Main and Second so the Indian children, Red Men, Chief Elkhart and Princess Mishawaka could join the procession. The Mishawaka Business Men's Association and others who organized the day's events were next, riding in automobiles. Following them were the Mishawaka Bugle Corps and the Presbyterian Cadets. The Grand Army of the Republic's float had a soldier standing at arms and a fife-and-drum player. The Woodmen of the World's entry had a log cabin surrounded by a rail fence, and in front of the house was an axe, the order's symbol. The Knights of Pythias, Oddfellows and Rebekahs also had entries, and the Mishawaka Fire Department's decorated wagons brought up the rear.

The theme of an "industrial pageant" became more evident with the second division. The city's largest industry, Mishawaka Woolen, was the first business represented in the parade. Its fire brigade preceded a dozen floats that represented the company's different departments. The most memorable Ball-Band entries were the shipping department's wagon with a fourteen-foot-high load of boxes and the float with the corporate emblem and advertising slogan, which consisted of a rubber snake, symbolizing the trusts, trying to eat a frog, standing for Mishawaka Woolen. Continuing the footwear theme, the John A. Herzog Shoe Store float displayed a ten-foot-long concrete shoe, made by the Concrete Manufacturing & Construction Company, and several little girls enacting the Mother Goose story of the old woman who lived in a shoe. Other businesses' floats followed, including Perkins Wind Mill Company's display of a windmill turned by a gas engine and Ripple Milling Company's depiction of how milling had changed over time. Beatty Felting Company and Roper Furniture Company exhibited their products. Major Brothers Packing Company had six floats and pleased the crowd by throwing hot wieners!

The third division was headlined by Dodge Manufacturing, which had fourteen entries. The company had gone to the expense of commissioning Chicago artists, who spent weeks painting scenes depicting the business's growth and development. Dodge's representation also included its band, the fire department and automobiles carrying men who had been employed by the company for twenty-five or more years. Following Dodge were Simplex Motor Car Company's float, bearing a 1909 touring car filled with little girls; three National Veneer Products Company entries;

The Mishawaka Woolen Manufacturing Company floats in the parade. *Mishawaka-Penn-Harris Public Library.*

and several other businesses, such as Mishawaka Trust & Savings, its float made to look like a large safe.

The fourth division included Tribune Printing Company's float with a huge pile of paper rolls and a sign stating that five miles of paper was used to print each day's Mishawaka edition. Plumber John Distler's entry featured a modern bathroom and a boy in his nightgown washing in the bathtub. Kamm & Schellinger Brewing Company came next, followed by Finch & Sprague Undertakers' ambulance, its horses covered in blankets made of beautiful flowers. Other businesses' entries included First National Bank, First Trust & Savings, Red Cross Pharmacy and Home Telephone Company, which had a float consisting of ten phones ranging in size from small to large.

Beiger Furniture Company's entries may have made the biggest sensation. They depicted two completely furnished rooms and a sign that said the couple in the living room would be married at noon. The company had run a newspaper ad that offered a $100 bedroom suite to the first couple who would agree to get married on the Beiger float. Ernest Hoover and Agnes Willard, both of Wakarusa, accepted the offer. Agnes wore white and

Dodge Manufacturing Company had numerous floats in the Independence Day parade. *Mishawaka-Penn-Harris Public Library.*

a bridal veil, and they sat on the couch during the parade route as men with megaphones continually announced their impending nuptials. The *Weekly Times* later reported, "A great crowd was present at the corner of Fourth and Main Streets" when a justice of the peace performed the ceremony.

The fifth division featured the Wakarusa Band, the Klondike Band and a chariot drawn by four horses. Among the businesses included were Weber Kash Grocery, De La Claire Manufacturing Company, Perkins Electric Company, Fisher Harness Company, Clark's Laundry, *South Bend News*, Red Line Delivery and the Economy Bazaar.

Despite a steady drizzle, huge numbers of people turned out to watch the spectacle, which stretched for more than three miles and took nearly an hour to pass. Although crowd estimates for such an event are difficult to make, the *Enterprise* later referred to the "many thousands of visitors who thronged the line of march." The *Tribune* referred to an amazing figure of "40,000 people at the homecoming," most of whom would have watched the parade or been participants in it, and described the parade as "the greatest pageant ever seen in Mishawaka or northern Indiana." Historian Vincent Brunner, the aide who directed the second division, later estimated that twenty thousand people traveled to Mishawaka for the day's events.

The drama and pageantry of the morning would have been exciting and memorable enough, but the day's events were only getting started. Soon after the parade ended, all eyes were directed to the corner of Third and Main. At noon, Princess Mishawaka, Chief Elkhart, the Indian children and thousands of onlookers gathered in front of the Hotel Mishawaka. The princess and chief walked up the steps. "Holding the ropes in her hands," wrote the *News*, "the Princess tugged with her slender, dimpled hands, and the green and gold pennant of the city railed slowly to the flag staff and nestled along side the Stars and Stripes. The new hotel had been formally opened." Hundreds dined in the hotel for the first time that afternoon and evening. With thousands of visitors strolling through the attractive building, the registered guests had to wait several more hours before they could enjoy the peace and relaxation of their accommodations.

To keep the large crowds entertained, various events were held in the afternoon at venues on both sides of the river. At 1:00 p.m., a balloon ascension occurred at the foot of Main Street near the south race. At 1:30 p.m., the doubles tennis tournament took place at Third and Union.

Hotel Mishawaka, circa 1909. *Author's collection.*

Between 1:30 and 3:00 p.m., the intersection of Main and Joseph was the scene of sporting events that included a 100-yard dash, a girls' race (age eighteen and under), an old man's race (over age fifty), a two-mile marathon, a three-legged race, a wheelbarrow race, a standing broad jump, a bicycle race and a married woman's race. At the same time, other events were held on the south side of the river, including a greased pig contest, a sack race, a fat man's race (two hundred pounds and over), a 50-yard dash for women, a boys' race, tug-of-war and a roller-skating race.

While these events were primarily for fun, the winners also received prizes offered by local merchants. Several top finishers received boxes of cigars. Examples of other prizes included a one-year subscription to the *South Bend Tribune*, a clock from Parmenter Jewelry, photos taken by Ostrander Photography, a pair of shoes from Williams & Myers, four suits pressed by Rubeshaw Suitatorium, two tons of coal from Russell the Coal Man and a ham from Fred Major's meat market. Participants in the girls' race were motivated by a hat from Miss Carpenter & Company or perfume from Robinson & McFarland Drug Store, and the winner of the married woman's race took home a gas stove to be installed by the South Bend and Mishawaka Gas Company. The biggest prize of all, though, went to the winning eight-man tug-of-war team: an eight-gallon beer keg from Kamm & Schellinger.

At 3:00 p.m., the most prominent event of the afternoon's sports program was held: a twenty-two-mile motorcycle race starting at Church Street along Second Street to a point two miles south of Elkhart and back, finishing at Cedar Street. The ten participants were released at one-minute intervals and their times compared. The winner completed the course in 33:40 despite being thrown twenty-five feet from his bike while going over a railroad crossing in Osceola. The top three finishers were awarded, respectively, a motorcycle lamp; goggles and gauntlets; and a box of cigars.

Just as the athletic contests were winding down, an audience of two thousand gathered in Battell Park at 3:00 p.m. Fifty children from St. Joseph School costumed as Indians, likely the same tribe from the morning's pageant, put on a fifteen-minute "drill" enacting their rendition of native dances. Congressman Henry Barnhart was the featured speaker for the event. In what the *News* described as a "short but vigorous address," Barnhart noted that the children's performance was a reminder of the ordeals endured by the pioneers so that later generations could enjoy peace and prosperity, which he challenged the audience to value and safeguard. Representative Barnhart also spoke of the importance of honesty in public life and asserted that the day's events were a patriotic occasion and an opportunity to teach this belief to every citizen, regardless of party affiliation. The Mishawaka City Band then entertained the crowd.

More activities continued into the late afternoon. At 4:00 p.m., Conn's Band, from Elkhart, performed at the intersection of Main and Joseph; at the same time, Reese's Band played at Church and Second, and the LaPorte City Band gave a concert on the veranda of the Hotel Mishawaka. At 5:00 p.m., Otis Johnson made another dive from the ladder atop the Ripple Milling Company, and Mme. Alferretti did her trapeze and rings act at Main and Third. At 6:30 p.m., a second balloon ascension and parachute drop occurred, the daredevil landing safely near the river bank along the 100 block of West Joseph.

At 7:00 p.m., all of the bands gathered together into "one grand band of 100 pieces and they marched up Main Street amid the enthusiasm of the people," the *Tribune* wrote.

The front steps of the Hotel Mishawaka were again the center of attention at 8:00 p.m. as five thousand people, according to the *Times*, filled Main Street from Second to Fourth and Third Street between Church and Mill. They had come to witness the ceremony in which the new electric streetlights would be formally turned over to the city and lit for the first time.

The keynote speaker, William O'Neill, addressed the assemblage, first commenting on the hotel's significance and then highlighting Melville Mix's role in its completion:

> *Today is an epoch-marking day in the history of our beautiful city. It marks the realization of long-cherished plans, the fruition which bears splendid testimony to the public spirit of our people and the propitious conditions under which we live.*
>
> *The magnificent structure in the shade of which we stand, the crowning glory of a decade of achievement, would do credit to a community many times the size of our city. It will do more to make Mishawaka pleasantly remembered from coast to coast than any other single institution in the city.*

O'Neill proceeded to offer a portrait of Mishawaka fifteen years earlier to show its dramatic growth. He noted the city's smaller population and boundaries, its modest industries and churches and the inadequate facilities for transportation and municipal government. While acknowledging "the limitations of the Mishawaka of that day," O'Neill also remembered the "sturdy citizenship" of men like Wallace Dodge, Martin Beiger, Adolphus Eberhart, Reverend August Oechtering, Edward Jernegan and others who had enabled Mishawaka's rise and progress. He then depicted the Mishawaka of 1909 and the growth in population and advances in industries, streets and bridges, fire and police departments, electric power and other areas of civic life. O'Neill also pointed to the new Mishawaka High School that would soon be built and the city's many new attractive houses of worship to prove that "prosperity has not lowered our ideals" or "appreciation of the finer and nobler things of life."

O'Neill ended with an appeal to the city's visitors to move to Mishawaka and "help us to realize our prophecy of 25,000 population in 1915." He offered this lofty and poetic vision of the life that could be had in Mishawaka:

Nowhere is the sunshine brighter, nowhere is the bird's song sweeter, nowhere is the grass greener or heaven's vaulted canopy a more enchanting blue than in this city of beauty and industry and opportunity...

Come then and have a home, in all that the word implies, in a city of such promise, where labor finds profitable employment, where the employer knows his man, and the old-time feeling of mutual respect and esteem exists between them, where your children may enjoy educational advantages unsurpassed in the country and your family the conveniences and comforts of city life with few of the disadvantages usually attendant thereon. Come and you will find the door of opportunity ajar, and as you become one of us, you may have her inspiring assurance that in this community men are esteemed for what they are rather than for what they have, that a decent, industrious, well-ordered life, however humble its beginning, places the citizen far above the reach of the detractor or calumniator and secures for him that prize guerdon of citizenship, the respect and affectionate regard of his neighbors.

The city attorney then introduced the president of the Mishawaka Business Men's Association, John Herzog, who began his brief remarks by asserting that his organization's "splendid gift" of the lighting system spoke "eloquently...of their public spirit and generosity." Formally presenting the streetlights to the city, Herzog stated that it was "as an earnest of our interest in city affairs and a pledge of our continued support of all laudable city projects."

Mayor Frank received the lighting system and, on behalf of the citizens, expressed his appreciation and gratitude. Frank then remarked on how the lights exemplified what relations between city government and business owners should be like:

It is gratifying evidence of the harmony that exists between the business and property interests of the city and the municipal government, without which it is impossible to secure results, however well meant may be the efforts of your city officials. It is so much more profitable to cooperate with those in authority in securing the best city government obtainable than it is to stand idly by and criticize mistakes that too often are made solely on account of lack of public interest being shown at the proper time. I hope the time will never come in Mishawaka when there will be any abatement of the interest that is evidenced by this gift.

The mayor acknowledged the great expense the businessmen had incurred to install the lights and pledged that the city would fulfill its obligation of maintaining them "as a perpetual reminder of this great day in local history and of how its success was assured by harmonious and concerted effort on the part of the businessmen, manufacturers, and city authorities."

The crowd's anticipation grew as Princess Mishawaka was then escorted to the hotel veranda by Melville Mix. The *News* painted this verbal portrait of the scene and what unfolded next:

Her dusky profile silhouetted against the shady lawn where thousands stood at attention while to her left on the street in serried ranks stood 150 pieces of brass instruments awaiting the signal. There was a moment's pause and then a dazzling glare of light. Miss Skelly had turned the switch and the new lighting system had been formally opened. And as huzzas roared from the throats of thousands, the 150 instruments blared forth "The Star Spangled Banner" that caused the audience to cheer and clap as the pretty Mishawaka girl, holding aloft the flag of her country and the pennant of her city, beat time as the national song burst forth on the summer air.

"The effect was magical," wrote the *Weekly Times*. "With one long shout the citizens…greeted the event." The *Tribune*'s reporter got caught up in the excitement of the moment as he described the "blaze of glory" and noted, "The enthusiasm spread over the city and cheers could be heard for miles." At 8:45 p.m., an "illuminated automobile parade" traveled along brightly lit Joseph, Main and Second Streets.

The original plans for the homecoming celebration called for an enormous fireworks display from the Cedar Street Bridge to celebrate the nation's birthday. Four thousand people gathered on Edgewater Drive and Second Street, but they were soon disappointed to hear that due to the dampness from the morning's rain, the expert from the National Fireworks Company insisted on postponing until drier conditions allowed the powder to ignite properly and the pyrotechnics to explode at a safe height. The fireworks show was rescheduled for Thursday evening and advertised as "Carnival Night in Mishawaka," a belated encore to Mishawaka's Independence Day celebration. The *Enterprise* later reported that "many thousands" enjoyed the "splendid exhibit" and then "roamed the streets inspecting our brilliant new lighting system, the new hotel and other attractions."

Other than the rain during the parade and the fireworks postponement, the day went exceptionally well. There were no serious accidents or fires and little drunkenness or disorder. In fact, the quietest place in town was the jail, which remained empty all day and night. The police, though, did confiscate "over a half bushel" of revolvers, reported the *Enterprise*, as it was against the law to fire those weapons in the city. All in all, declared the paper, "It was a record to be proud of as a municipality."

Mishawaka and its neighboring cities of South Bend and Elkhart were often rivals in pursuing new businesses, but all that was set aside on July 5. The South Bend Chamber of Commerce had unselfishly urged its members and all citizens to support and attend Mishawaka's celebration. And they did. Fifteen thousand passengers traveled by streetcar from South Bend to Mishawaka that day. The Elkhart interurban office reported that it sold 1,200 tickets to Mishawaka, and another three hundred passengers came via the Lake Shore & Michigan Southern Railroad.

After the decorations came down, the visitors went home and the last of the fireworks burst in the night sky, the legacy of July 5, 1909, lived on in different ways, even into the twenty-first century. The electric streetlights donated by the Mishawaka Business Men's Association brought modernity to downtown and evidenced the city's commitment to a better quality of life. Those original lights have been replaced several times over the years, and now electric lights are on every street in the city. Mishawaka residents today are so used to electric streetlights that it takes great effort to imagine a time when thousands cheered and bands played because the lights came on.

The other focus of attention during the homecoming celebration was the Hotel Mishawaka, which endured for decades as one of the city's outstanding buildings. Due to declining business, the Hotel Mishawaka went into receivership in 1923 and was sold, the first of several times the building changed hands. By the 1950s, the hotel had sixty guest rooms, a banquet room, a dining room, a cocktail lounge, a beauty shop, a barbershop, the Mishawaka Chamber of Commerce offices and even a radio station. In addition to accommodating thousands of guests over the years, the hotel was also a venue for service club meetings and other community events. By the early 1960s, the Hotel Mishawaka faced foreclosure and needed an expensive renovation. City leaders were also caught up in urban renewal mania and wanted to clear the block where the hotel stood to make way for a civic center. This combination of circumstances proved fatal, and the Hotel Mishawaka was razed in May 1968. A new post office was built on the site and dedicated in June 1970. The hotel's demolition still evokes grief, anger and dismay half a century later.

The Hotel Mishawaka lives on, though, through photographs, postcards and other advertising ephemera. The largest artifact from the hotel is a painting depicting French explorer Robert Cavelier de La Salle's landing in Mishawaka. Edmund Philo Kellogg, a Chicago muralist, was commissioned to do the six-by-nine-foot painting for the Hotel Mishawaka, where it was first hung over the lobby's fireplace mantel on July 5, 1909. The painting was saved from the wrecking ball, cleaned and restored by Ray Chamberlin, hung in the old city hall and moved to the present city hall in 1986. It hangs just outside the council chamber, yet few people today realize that the La Salle painting is the last surviving witness to the grand opening of the Hotel Mishawaka.

The rotunda of the Hotel Mishawaka is shown in this postcard, made shortly after the hotel opened. Note the La Salle painting hanging over the fireplace. *Author's collection.*

The organizers of the Independence Day and homecoming events asserted their belief in "All for Mishawaka," regardless of where in the city one lived, and established the goal of 25,000 residents by 1915. Mishawaka soon outgrew whatever intracity rivalries once existed and lived up to the mantra stated on the cloverleaf buttons and signs. As for the 1915 population goal, Mishawaka fell substantially short, reaching 11,864 in the 1910 U.S. Census and only 15,195 in 1920. World War I and postwar economic problems curtailed the immigration that had been driving the local population boom. The city did eventually reach the 25,000 milestone and had 28,581 residents by 1930, leading the entire state in growth percentage during the 1920s. Mishawaka's population has never again increased so much so fast, but it has enjoyed steady growth over the decades. The 2020 U.S. Census may well show that Mishawaka has 50,000 citizens, an achievement that would surely amaze and please Charles Frank, William O'Neill and John Herzog.

The Independence Day celebration of 1909 has influenced posterity in other ways too. Mishawakans still like a good fireworks display, especially when they are surrounded by thousands of their neighbors. Many recall fondly the July 4 fireworks shows at Wilson Park in the 1970s, and enormous crowds today fill Central Park to witness the city's annual Independence Day fireworks extravaganza. Much like their great-grandparents and great-great-grandparents in 1909, Mishawakans also love a parade. Over the years, the city has held many of these celebratory processions, including parades that sent soldiers off to war in 1917, a large parade in 1932 for Mishawaka's centennial, homecoming parades for Mishawaka High School and a bicentennial parade in 1976. For the past seventy years, the Mishawaka Memorial Day Parade has been a cherished tradition. Although not an "industrial pageant," the parade still features several marching bands, many civic organizations and a few local businesses. The 2019 parade had ninety entries, and more than ten thousand people lined the city's streets to view the spectacle.

As the Memorial Day parade's line of march goes down Main Street, it partly retraces the route traveled by Princess Mishawaka, Chief Elkhart, Ball-Band and Dodge floats and so many others in 1909. Listening carefully amid the parade's music, sirens and applause, one might just hear the faint echoes of a ghostly crowd on a glorious day long ago.

Chapter 4

Picturing History

Mishawaka Recruits and World War I

W hen Meijer opened its Bremen Highway store in 1995, the company sought to establish a connection to Mishawaka by permanently displaying seven large historic photographs from the collection of the Mishawaka-Penn-Harris Public Library, each measuring roughly four by five feet.

The most compelling of these photos is of a group of men standing in front of the U.S. Post Office building at 120 South Church Street. Handwritten along the bottom of the image is this wording:

> *Recruits*
> *Leaving May 10.17.*
> *Mishawaka, Ind.*

The student of history will recall that the European powers had been fighting World War I since August 1914, but American involvement began with a declaration of war on April 6, 1917. The men in the Meijer photo were thus some of the first U.S. Army recruits from Mishawaka to participate in the war.

Mishawakans should learn how that image came to be and what happened to those eager, patriotic volunteers who stared across a century at the shoppers in checkout lane no. 12.

Long before the United States officially entered the war, some Mishawakans were already in harm's way. The first Mishawaka men to leave for the Great War were fifteen Belgian reservists who had been recalled by the Belgian government to resist Germany's invasion of the small neutral country. They left on September 20, 1914, bidden farewell by a band and several hundred people at the New York Central railroad depot. Jacques Vander Haden and Edward Rogiers, two Belgian soldiers, were the first Mishawakans killed in World War I. Vander Haden died in Belgium on July 9, 1917, as a result of wounds from a German bomb. In mid-September, Rogiers's family learned that he had died in France. Aware that the United States could be pulled into the war at any time, other local men joined the peacetime American armed forces.

For almost three years, the American people had read about atrocities committed by the German army and violations of maritime rights by the German navy, and they worried what would happen to Europe and civilization itself if the Central Powers (Germany, the Austro-Hungarian Empire and the Ottoman Empire) were to win the war of attrition against Britain, France and the rest of the Allied Powers.

After Congress declared war, Mishawaka men eagerly answered the call by volunteering for the army and navy. John Herzog, the Mishawaka postmaster, signed the enlistment papers of some of the earliest recruits until Corporal G.E. Bonshire arrived on April 24 to open a temporary recruiting station in the basement of the post office, also referred to as the "federal building."

On May 1, a contingent of twenty-five army recruits from Mishawaka was given a public send-off on the front steps of the post office. In his comments before a large crowd, Herzog praised the recruits for their patriotism. He was followed with remarks by Reverend Louis Moench of St. Joseph Church, Reverend G.W. Titus of the First Christian Church and Mayor Ralph Gaylor. A parade to the railroad depot included a platoon of police, the Mishawaka Woolen Manufacturing Company band, Corporal Bonshire and the recruits, mail carriers in uniform, Mishawaka Woolen employees, Mayor Gaylor and citizens on foot and in automobiles. After the recruits left Mishawaka, they traveled to Fort Wayne for further examination before being sent to Fort Thomas, Kentucky.

In the following days, even more Mishawaka men came to the recruiting station, which stayed open until nine o'clock each evening to handle the surge of enlistees. Thirty-two recruits signed up on Wednesday, May 2, the day after the parade, and another twenty joined on Thursday. Nine more were added to the rolls on Saturday, fourteen on Monday and eight more before the *Mishawaka Enterprise* went to press on Friday, May 11.

The patriotic fervor sweeping across the city was also felt at Mishawaka High School. On the evening of May 7, the Booster Club and student council sponsored a farewell celebration for math teacher and athletic director Charles Semler and several students who had enlisted. Speeches by Superintendent D.W. Horton and Principal Daniel Eikenberry, dancing and patriotic songs were part of the event. Four months later, Eikenberry would also enlist, serving as educational director of the YMCA facility at Camp Shelby in Hattiesburg, Mississippi.

Recruits continued pouring into the Mishawaka Post Office, so the army and town officials began planning another, even larger send-off for the afternoon of May 10.

For more than an hour, all other activity in Mishawaka came to a standstill as the community showed its patriotism and honored the seventy-six recruits leaving for war. To encourage participation in the day's festivities, schoolchildren were dismissed until 2:00 p.m., and many local businesses closed at noon so employees could gather in front of the post office. Under a cloudless blue sky and warm sun, the gathering grew large. The *South Bend News-Times* referred to "thousands of people" participating in or spectating at the event. The *Enterprise* and the *South Bend Tribune* described the assemblage as a "vast throng" and "great throng," respectively.

While citizens were arriving before the noon starting time, patriotic music wafted down from the chimes of the Methodist Episcopal Church, just across East Third Street.

Local merchants provided the recruits with cigars and tobacco, and Charles Ostrander, Mishawaka's leading commercial and portrait photographer, took a photo of the men on the post office's front steps before the program of speakers began.

Postmaster Herzog opened with a few brief remarks before presenting Mayor Gaylor as the chairman for the event. Among his comments, Gaylor stated, "This is another proud day in the history of Mishawaka, and this is an indication that patriotism is not on a low ebb here."

He proceeded to introduce the other speakers, which included Reverend Dr. John Burnett, pastor of the First Presbyterian Church and president of the local American Red Cross; Reverend John Bleckmann, pastor of St. Monica's Church; Edward Jernegan, Civil War veteran and editor of the *Enterprise*; Adna Warner, general manager of Mishawaka Woolen; Edwin Ahara, superintendent of the Dodge Manufacturing Company; and Captain Thomas Ryan, who commanded the Fort Wayne district recruiting station and would escort the Mishawaka volunteers to Fort Wayne for further examination.

Charles Ostrander photographed the recruits who left Mishawaka on May 10, 1917.
Mishawaka-Penn-Harris Public Library.

The *Enterprise* and *Tribune* accounts devoted the most space to summarizing Captain Ryan's remarks. He told the crowd that the war was not President Wilson's war, nor was it being fought because hundreds of American lives had been lost on the high seas. Rather, it was a war for democracy. Ryan told the recruits that they should leave Mishawaka with their heads held high, knowing that when they returned "it will be with victory inscribed on their banner." He praised Mishawakans for their patriotism and cooperation, noting that the city had already given Uncle Sam two hundred volunteers.

Other speakers expressed patriotic sentiments, motivating both the recruits and the citizenry for the challenges that lay ahead. Reverend Bleckmann shared his belief that the Mishawaka volunteers would help fulfill Lincoln's "prophecy" from the Gettysburg Address that "this nation shall have a new birth of freedom." Jernegan said the occasion stirred the hearts of old soldiers such as him by giving proof that patriotism was not dead. The *Tribune* said that Warner and Ahara "wished the recruits Godspeed on their mission." Reverend Burnett explained that the local Red Cross would soon be mobilized, ready to help the soldiers and their families in any way needed.

After the speakers finished, a parade departed the post office at 12:30 p.m., led by Jason J. Davis, a Spanish-American War veteran and a reporter for the *News-Times*, who was on horseback. Following Davis was the entire Mishawaka police force, the Dodge Manufacturing band in full uniform, Ryan and Herzog and then the seventy-six recruits. Continuing the procession behind them were twenty-five girls from the high school wearing Red Cross outfits, the Eberhart Drum Corps, Civil War veterans, the Boy Scouts drum corps and other Boy Scouts in uniform. Mayor Gaylor and Reverend Bleckmann were at the rear of the official procession. Following them were hundreds of citizens, marching on foot or riding in automobiles. Students walking in the parade were each given a small American flag to carry.

The parade's line of march continued north on Church Street, past Lincolnway to First Street, west to Main Street, south to Lincolnway, west to Mill Street and south on Mill three blocks to the New York Central depot.

As large as the crowd was in front of the post office, the *Enterprise* estimated that a "bigger crowd massed at the railway station when the boys departed." The *News-Times* added this descriptive detail of the scene: "Freight cars standing in the vicinity were covered with school boys who made merry with singing while the crowd was waiting for the train."

According to the *Tribune* account, there stood "the boys amid the cheers of the large number gathered there to say good bye and God speed as the train pulled out at 12:55 p.m. Many touching scenes were enacted as mothers, sisters, and sweethearts said a good by while tears coursed down their cheeks. It will be a scene long remembered in the history of Mishawaka."

The Mishawakans' train reached Fort Wayne at about 3:00 p.m., reported the *Fort Wayne Journal-Gazette*, which praised the men's bearing upon arriving in the Summit City: "The recruits formed in parade line at the depot and marched to the army office, where they were examined and accepted in various branches of the service. The Mishawaka young men composed one of the finest bunches of recruits enlisted here since the outbreak of the war."

That afternoon's *Tribune* article about the parade and send-off included the headlines "Big Demonstration for Young Patriots" and "Great Outpouring of People Sees Boys Off." The story began by saying, "The biggest demonstration of its kind ever held in Mishawaka took place at noon to-day when the populace turned out en masse to pay its tribute to the 75 young patriots."

The *News-Times* described the event as "the greatest farewell demonstration that has ever been witnessed here, not even excepting Civil War days."

The next day's issue of the *Enterprise* swelled with civic pride over the farewell to the recruits: "Again has Mishawaka demonstrated her loyalty and patriotism by furnishing another detachment of 76 brave young volunteers for the war. This company, added to the previous number of recruits reported, makes a total of over 200 soldiers already furnished by our loyal little city, and sets a record which will be difficult to beat by any other community in the nation. The farewell send-off given by our citizens yesterday noon to the volunteers was a public demonstration worthy of the city and a proud testimonial to the loyal recruits."

The pageantry and emotion of the May 10, 1917 demonstration were captured most enduringly by the Ostrander photo, taken shortly before the program and parade that sent the seventy-six Mishawakans off to military service. The image includes recruits standing in roughly five rows, the first on the bottom step. All but one of the men is wearing a suit and tie, and most also have on a hat or cap. Two men in uniform are seated on the bottom step, their feet on the sidewalk. The man to the left wears sergeant's stripes, and the other soldier is likely Captain Ryan. Most men in the photo are looking at the camera, but a dozen on the right side of the group are glancing off to the right, perhaps reacting to a particularly spirited cheer from near the northwest corner of Church and Third. Several recruits are smiling, two seem to be yelling, nine are holding American flags on sticks and one man has a cigar in his mouth. Five signs are visible in the photograph. One is on a stick held by a young man in the back row and includes the words "ENLIST NOW" below what appear to be other lines too faint to read. Three men in the front right of the group are holding a large hand-lettered sign that reads:

WE'RE FROM
AND FOR
MISHAWAKA
AND THE GOOD OLD
U.S.A.

Behind and to the right is a sign leaning against a light post with the word "WANTED" readable at the top. Other lines show a number—possibly 100,000—and the words "VOLUNTEERS" and "U.S. ARMY." An apparently identical sign rests against the other light post but is mostly blocked by the men standing in front of it. The largest sign is a dark banner hanging from a pole above the building's front entrance. In white letters, it says:

Men Wanted
In the
United States
Army

The wording is only visible because a gust of wind from the north blew the banner at an angle, revealing the message and adding a hint of movement to the image. Shadows from the bare branches of an unseen tree stretch across the sidewalk in the lower right corner, suggesting a sunny spring day.

The words "Ostrander, Photo" are written in white below the first step on the right side of the picture. None of the gathered well-wishers appears in the photo, and the sidewalk in front of the men is clear all the way to the bottom of the image, close to the street curb. To get back far enough to include the entire group of volunteers in his photo, Ostrander must have stood in the street, the spectators behind and to either side of him.

Newspaper coverage of the May 10 festivities specifically states that seventy-six recruits left town that day, and Captain Ryan's letter of thanks also uses that number. Subsequent articles from throughout the war often refer to individual soldiers as being part of the contingent of seventy-six enlistees who departed Mishawaka on May 10, 1917. Ostrander's photo, though, shows only sixty-four recruits. None of the local papers ran the photo in 1917 with a caption identifying which men were in the image, and one is left to speculate why only sixty-four men appear in the picture. The *Enterprise* of May 11 listed names in four cohorts: forty-eight men in the first, with the acknowledgment that two names were not included; nine men who enlisted on May 5; fourteen more from May 7; and finally eight recruits who are referred to as "subsequent enlistments." These numbers total eighty-one men who volunteered during the period of May 1–10. The May 10 issue of the *News-Times*, though, lists the names of exactly seventy-six recruits who departed Mishawaka on May 10.

Charles Ostrander later loaned his photo to the *Mishawaka Enterprise*, which published it on May 11, 1925, under the headline "An Echo of Those Stirring Days." The caption included forty-seven names—all but one man listed in the group of forty-eight published in 1917—but they were not identified individually in the photo. In fact, the paper tried unsuccessfully to do so, saying, "It is a significant commentary upon what eight years will do when it is stated that it was impossible to find anyone who could identify any more than ten or 15 of them now." The same photo was reprinted in the *Enterprise* on April 2 and 9, 1998, and a reader, A.J. King, was able to identify his father, Thomas G. King, and uncle, Clem C. Coll, in the front row behind the uniformed soldiers.

The 76 recruits who departed Mishawaka on May 10, 1917, were not the first men from the Princess City to answer President Wilson's call that "the world must be made safe for democracy," nor would they be the last. A July 1918 *Tribune* article stated that 950 Mishawakans, including 600 volunteers, were in the army, and others had joined the navy. By war's end, more than 1,000 Mishawaka men had served in the armed forces. Some never left the United States, but most went "over there," mainly to France, where the doughboys saw intense fighting during the last five months of the war. In total, 33 Mishawaka men died in World War I, some from disease or accident, others killed in action or as a result of wounds received in combat. Over a dozen were wounded, a few were injured by poison gas and one spent the conflict's final four months as a prisoner of war.

Five of the May 10 enlistees died in service to their country: Paul Oppelt, Joseph Van de Putte, Firmin Van Holsbeck, Donald Bryan and Floyd Godfrey. Each man's story represents some of the experiences of his brothers-in-arms from Mishawaka during the Great War.

Twenty-one-year-old Corporal Paul Oppelt, a Dodge Manufacturing machinist, was in the 49th Infantry Regiment at Camp Merritt, New Jersey, and served as a guard at Pier No. 5 along the New Jersey shore of the Hudson River. He developed double pneumonia and died on March 28, 1918, in a Hoboken hospital. His brother Joseph, also a May 10 volunteer, was stationed at the same camp but was home on leave when he received the telegram about Paul's passing. Hundreds viewed the body in the Oppelt home at 701 East Fourth Street, and the funeral Mass at St. Joseph Church included pallbearers and escorts provided by the local home guards. Corporal Oppelt was laid to rest at St. Joseph Cemetery.

Private Joseph Van de Putte, age twenty-two, was the first May 10 recruit to be killed in action. A Belgian immigrant, Van de Putte was a machinist at Dodge Manufacturing and resided at 613 West Sixth Street. He served in the 16th Infantry Regiment, 1st Division, and was killed in France on June 6, 1918. According to the American Battle Monuments Commission, the location of his remains is unknown. Private Van de Putte is memorialized on the "Wall of the Missing" at Somme American Cemetery in northern France, not far from the Belgian border.

The same August 23 issue of the *Enterprise* that reported Van de Putte's death also informed the community of the loss of twenty-two-year-old Private Firmin Van Holsbeck. Like Van de Putte, he was born in Belgium

Firmin Van Holsbeck is buried at Aisne-Marne American Cemetery, France. *Author's collection.*

and worked in the machine shop at Dodge Manufacturing. Van Holsbeck lived at 407 West Ninth Street, belonged to the Belgian-American Club and had won many races as a member of the Belgian Bicycle Club. He originally had been part of the 30th Infantry and later was transferred to the 16th Infantry. After recovering from a severe case of diphtheria in England, Van Holsbeck went to France and was assigned to the 9th Infantry, 2nd Division. He was severely wounded at Soissons on July 15, the opening day of the Second Battle of the Marne, which was the last major German offensive on the Western Front. A nurse at the American Red Cross hospital in Paris wrote to Van Holsbeck's mother that Firmin had died from his wounds on July 21. A memorial service for Private Van Holsbeck was held at St. Bavo Church on Labor Day, and he was buried at Aisne-Marne American Cemetery, fifty miles northeast of Paris.

As the Allies pushed ever closer to Germany in the fall of 1918, the fighting in northern France reached a bloody crescendo and claimed the lives of two more Mishawakans from the May 10 cadre.

Corporal Donald Bryan died on October 9 from wounds received when crossing Dead Man's Hill near Thiacourt, two hundred miles east of Paris. Bryan, age twenty-two, was born near Argos, Indiana. Before enlisting, he worked at the Gillette Motor Car Company in Mishawaka and resided with his family at 205 South Spring Street. He had trained at Fort Thomas and was assigned to the 5th Engineers at Camp Scurry in Corpus Christi, Texas, before being sent to France in August 1918. According to Corporal F.R. McNabb, a Mishawaka man serving in the same unit, Bryan was one of the first in their regiment to be killed, the first night the 5th Engineers came within range of German artillery. Corporal Bryan was initially buried at Saint-Mihiel American Cemetery near Thiacourt, but his remains were reinterred at Oak Hill Cemetery in Plymouth, Indiana, in 1921.

Twenty-four-year-old Private Floyd Godfrey, serving with the 61st Infantry, 5th Division, died in France on October 12. Godfrey had lived in Mishawaka for the past decade, residing with his aunt and uncle at 113 North Mill Street, and worked at the Rubber Regenerating Company. Following his enlistment,

Godfrey was stationed in Syracuse, New York, and Charlotte, North Carolina, before arriving in England in April 1918. He saw bloody fighting in the Battle of Saint-Mihiel in September and the Meuse-Argonne Offensive in early October. His aunt, Allie Grim, initially learned that Floyd had been wounded on October 10 and admitted to a hospital on October 12, after which she received no communication from her nephew. In December 1918, the army's adjutant general informed the Grims that Floyd had died. Mrs. Grim's subsequent efforts to locate him or learn other details were fruitless until another telegram from the adjutant general in June 1919 confirmed

Floyd Godfrey's grave is in Fairview Cemetery, Mishawaka. *Author's collection.*

Godfrey's death. In February 1920, the army told the Grims that he had been killed in action on October 12. Private Godfrey's remains were returned to Mishawaka for burial at Fairview Cemetery in October 1921.

Other May 10 volunteers were wounded or injured during their service abroad, according to the local newspapers. Private Arthur Kelly of the 16th Infantry was severely wounded on July 19. Sergeant John Magolske of the 660th Aero Squadron was both gassed and badly wounded on November 11, the final day of fighting. He returned to a California hospital for prolonged and extensive rehabilitation. Cyril Auwenrogge also was wounded in the final weeks of the war. James Sweitzer, who served in the 83rd Field Artillery, was listed in the newspaper as being "slightly wounded." Private Thomas Sheets seemed to cheat death on multiple occasions during the fighting he saw at Chateau-Thierry, the Argonne Forest and Soissons. He was never wounded but did have a bullet fly through his coat sleeve and shrapnel take the heel off his shoe. Sergeant John Leyes suffered a broken kneecap during postwar occupation duty in Germany and was sent back to the United States.

Another casualty among the May 10 recruits was Musician 2nd Class Benjamin Fetters, who was captured by the Germans on July 24, 1918. Fetters, age twenty-four, lived with his parents at 205 West Eighth Street, worked in the shipping department at Mishawaka Woolen and played saxophone in the company band. Fetters had been stationed at Camp Greene in Charlotte and then Camp Merritt before arriving in England in April. He served as a musician with the 30th Infantry band, and his regiment saw fighting at Catigny, Chateau-Thierry and the Second Battle of the Marne. In combat, Fetters worked with the medical corps and carried wounded soldiers to safety. While doing such hazardous duty, he was taken prisoner at La Chamel. On August 21, the army told Ben's parents that he was missing in action. On September 9, they were informed that he was in a prisoner-of-war camp in Langensalza, Germany. While there, Fetters was able to send his family a few postcards, one of which stated that he was mainly surviving off hardtack given to him by French prisoners. He left Langensalza on December 17, stayed at another prison camp in Cassel until Christmas Day and was finally sent to Frankfurt, where he was given over to a Swiss military officer. Fetters eventually returned to his unit on January 7.

Soon after, Fetters's family received a letter dated January 8 in which he reassured them of his well-being and summarized what had happened since his last communication on October 12. "I am just fine," Ben wrote. "I am back with the band again. I just got back last night and I was right glad. Many times I thought I would never get among the fellows again. They sure did give me a great reception and royal welcome.…We are in a fine place now and everything is fine. I'm glad it's all over."

In a January 29 letter, Fetters's tone was much less exhilarated, as he revealed details of conditions in his prison camp following the armistice. He explained, "We had quite a bad time, too. They doubled the guard and got pretty rough. Believe me, the Germans were certainly bad losers." Fetters described living in damp, cold, lice- and flea-infested shacks and having his feet be cold and wet because of holes in his shoes. Far more terrible was an incident Fetters survived in which prisoners were shot by camp guards and passing German troops:

My last time under fire will never be forgotten. The prisoners in camp had a little shack made of old boards and canvass that they had bought and put up themselves, using it for a theater. After the signing of the armistice, they asked permission from the commander of the camp to tear it down, which was given. It was wet and cold and we started to use it for boards for a fire. It only seemed a moment after we had started to dismantle it when a platoon of Germans appeared just outside of the fence and opened fire on us, and as soon as they did, every guard around the camp started in shooting. I flopped immediately, pretended to be a dead one, and that's what saved me. When firing ceased, I counted 19 of my prison soldier friends dead. Thirty or more were wounded. There were not many Americans among them. It was cold-blooded murder. Oh, how I hate them! Thank the Lord I am out of their hands.

Musician Fetters served eight months with the American forces occupying Germany and was discharged from the army in August 1919, after which he returned home to his relieved family in Mishawaka.

In May 1920, Fetters married Bessie Frick in South Bend, where they raised three children and enjoyed nearly fifty-five years together until Ben's death in 1975. As a civilian, Fetters traded his army uniform for that of a U.S. Postal Service letter carrier, a job he held for thirty-seven years. He also served as commander of American Legion Post 50 and was a member of other veterans organizations. Ben and Bessie are buried at Southlawn Cemetery in South Bend.

After witnessing the horror and trauma of war, Ben Fetters was blessed with the full, long life that Paul Oppelt, Joseph Van de Putte, Firmin Van Holsbeck, Donald Bryan, Floyd Godfrey and so many others were denied.

Mishawakans in 1917 and 1918 would have found it difficult to imagine a time when people would not understand or care about the profound events of "the war to end all wars." The May 10, 1917 *South Bend Tribune* had asserted that the farewell scene at the railroad depot would be "long remembered in the history of Mishawaka." That may have been true for a generation or two, but World War I has gradually joined the ranks of the forgotten wars as nearly all people alive then have since died off. World War II saw a larger number of Americans in uniform and much worse destruction and loss of life. More recent conflicts in Vietnam, Iraq and Afghanistan have greater prominence in memory and the media than do the valor and sacrifices of doughboys on the Western Front so long ago.

Mishawaka waited a century before it specifically memorialized its servicemen who died in World War I.

The Great War was certainly on Mishawakans' minds, though, as they dedicated the Battell Park Band Shell on Memorial Day 1928. An attractive bronze plaque on the band shell reads:

DEDICATED TO THOSE OF
MISHAWAKA, INDIANA
WHO OFFERED THEIR
LIVES IN HUMANITY'S
DEFENSE IN THE WARS

Of the Nation and in
Memory of Those Who
Gave Their Last Full
Measure of Devotion.
May 30, 1928

The nonspecific phrasing of the plaque remembers both living veterans and war dead while also projecting this honor and remembrance onto the participants of future wars. Far more massive than the Civil War Soldiers' Monument in the east end of Battell Park, the band shell is actually the biggest war memorial in Mishawaka. Few, if any, audience members sitting there for a summer concert, though, realize they are looking at what is, in large part, a World War I monument.

Forty-two years later, another war memorial was erected near the Fifer Community Mausoleum in Fairview Cemetery by the local American Legion and Veterans of Foreign Wars posts. Although the Vietnam War was raging at the time, the inscription on the small monument could apply to all of the nation's war veterans, including the men who served in World War I:

Dedicated
May 30, 1970
In Memory of Those Who Served in the
Armed Forces of the United States.
The Sacrifices They Made and the Deeds
They Performed Shall Be Written in History.
May They Rest in Peace.

This memorial has been moved to Fairview's new veterans section along Main Street.

For many years, Mishawaka's dead from World War II, Korea, Vietnam and the Middle East have had their names inscribed on impressive plaques in the lobby of city hall, but no such tribute listed the dead from World War I. This decades-old oversight was finally rectified on November 11, 2018. On the 100th anniversary of Armistice Day, city leaders and numerous veterans unveiled a new plaque that listed each of the city's dead from the Great War.

Shortly after the plaque was dedicated in city hall, the Meijer on Bremen Highway removed its Mishawaka images as part of a storewide remodeling. It was as if the photo of the May 1917 recruits had served its purpose as the most visible and personal reminder of World War I in Mishawaka until the community fulfilled its obligation to officially honor the Mishawakans from that war who gave the last full measure of devotion for their country.

Meijer later donated several of the large historic photos to the Mishawaka Historical Museum, where they will someday hang. As visitors to the museum look upon the photo of the May 10 recruits, they will see a picture that is worth far more than a thousand words.

Chapter 5

A Stall in the Cow Barn

The Mishawaka Cavemen and the 1927 Basketball State Finals

The year was 1927: Charles Lindbergh flew solo across the Atlantic, Babe Ruth hit sixty home runs and the Mishawaka Cavemen played in the state finals of the Indiana high school basketball tournament. Over the years, Mishawaka High has sent athletic teams to the state finals in football, volleyball, cross country, wrestling and basketball. While Cavemen volleyball and wrestling state championships are still fresh in the community's memory, it is difficult to imagine that Mishawaka once played in the boys' basketball state finals. The first MHS team to win its way to an IHSAA state finals, the 1927 basketball team became known as "Mishawaka's Victory Team" and thrilled the community with excitement and pride.

Prior to the 1924–25 season, the Mishawaka basketball program had existed for twenty years but with little to show for it. Local sports historian Scott Shuler asserted that when Mishawaka High School and South Bend High School played against each other in January 1904 it was "the very first basketball contest between two high schools in St. Joseph County." South Bend was victorious, setting a precedent for the schools' athletic relations.

South Bend was selected to participate in the 1913 state tourney and reached the championship game. The next year, the IHSAA changed the tourney format and invited all seventy-seven teams to compete in Bloomington. Mishawaka defeated Swayzee and Albion before bowing out with a loss to New Albany.

The open tourney format proved too unwieldy and was replaced by a series of "district," later called "sectional," tournaments in which the winners would advance to the state finals. In 1921, a regional round was added to reduce the state finals qualifiers to sixteen.

None of these changes had much effect on Mishawaka because the team failed to win any sectional titles. Dwelling in the shadow of South Bend, which reached four state finals between 1918 and 1923, the Maroon and White was a perennial also-ran in the local tourney. Even when Mishawaka and Lakeville met for the sectional title in 1924, it was Lakeville that emerged victorious.

Mishawaka and South Bend's intense civic rivalry was long-established, and the two towns now used high school sports to express their mutual dislike. Although Mishawaka struggled in basketball, it enjoyed better fortunes in football. Mishawaka defeated South Bend in 1920 and went on to claim a mythical state championship. When Frank Steele was named Mishawaka's coach in 1924, the glory years of Mishawaka football continued. The Cavemen defeated their archrival three consecutive years and claimed mythical state titles in 1925 and 1926.

Mishawaka sought to transfer its gridiron success to the hardwood. After three different coaches in four years, Shelby Shake was hired as the new basketball coach in 1924. Born and raised near Eminence in Morgan County, Shake graduated from Eminence High School and Indiana State Normal and served as an infantryman in the First World War. He had been a teacher and the basketball coach at Cloverdale High School for two years.

In 1923, at age twenty-seven, Shake came to Mishawaka as a woodshop and commercial math teacher.

Shake quickly built a reputation as one of the area's best coaches. Innovative and driven to win, he was known for rigorous practices, firm discipline and complex offensive and defensive schemes. Shake developed his players into what the *Miskodeed* described as "a smooth running machine." He also was a showman, employing tactics that inspired his team and intimidated opponents.

With Steele in charge of the football program and Shake taking the basketball reins, Mishawaka had outstanding coaches who could lead its teams to sustained success.

The 1926 *Miskodeed* included this photo of Coach Shelby Shake. *Mishawaka Historical Museum.*

A new school on Lincolnway East with modern facilities and a surging enrollment offered other factors in Mishawaka's favor. The Cavemen now had all the resources needed to challenge South Bend's athletic dominance. The town's slogan at the time—"Mishawaka, the city with the will and the power to do"—had also become the animating spirit behind its high school sports teams.

Shake's tenure as coach began inauspiciously as the Cavemen lost the first seven games of the 1924–25 campaign before rattling off a six-game winning streak. Mishawaka still could not get past South Bend and dropped both regular season contests to the Bears. Shake's plan for finally defeating the "Benders" was helped when Mishawaka's new gymnasium was named host site for the sectional, which previously had been contested at the YMCA in South Bend. The Cavemen had their revenge by beating South Bend in the semis, 17–15, and dominating Lakeville, 39–7, to win Mishawaka's first sectional crown. After an overtime loss to LaPorte in the regional, the Cavemen closed their season with a 12-11 record.

The Mishawaka High School gymnasium, pictured here when the new school opened in 1924, was the setting for the Cavemen's 1925 and 1927 sectional championships. *Mishawaka Historical Museum.*

By winning the sectional at South Bend's expense, Shake and his men had taken the Mishawaka–South Bend basketball rivalry to new heights. The schools split their regular season match-ups the following year, and Mishawaka took a 12-7 record into the sectional. Perhaps trying to intimidate the Orange and Blue, Shake ran up the scores on his first- and second-round opponents, defeating Center Township by a whopping 106–4 and Madison Township by 51–3. The favored Cavemen were spent, overconfident or a bit of both and fell to South Bend, 26–25, in the championship game.

The bitter defeat weighed on the mind of the intensely competitive Shake during the off season. The *Miskodeed* ended its season recap with a vow: "There's another year, South Bend."

With key players returning for the 1926–27 season, Mishawaka fans eagerly awaited what they hoped would be the school's best basketball season yet. The second-year captain of the senior-dominated team was Cy Himschoot. Among the great Mishawaka athletes of his era, Himschoot also starred on the Cavemen's state championship football teams. Other seniors included Burt Doyle, Al Eminger, Gordon Weist, Bob Hartzog, Harold Bennett and Francis "Frenchy" Denman. Himschoot, Doyle and Eminger had all played on Shake's sectional-winning team of 1925.

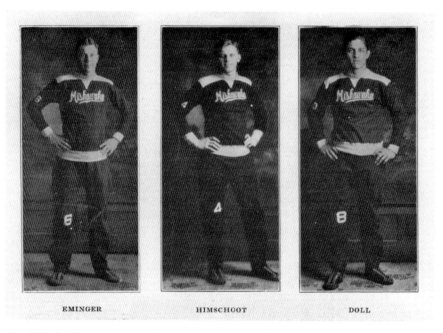

EMINGER   HIMSCHOOT   DOLL

The *Miskodeed* featured photos of members of the 1927 Cavemen basketball team. *Mishawaka Historical Museum.*

Junior center Ray DeCook had been on the varsity since he was a freshman. On his way to becoming one of the most successful basketball players in Mishawaka history, DeCook would lead the 1926–27 team in scoring. Ellsworth "Toad" Doll, Jimmy Gosbin and Lloyd Butz were the team's other juniors. Loaded with talent and experience, Mishawaka would be the team to beat if they lived up to expectations.

Shake's Cavemen opened their season with three consecutive victories. Making an early demonstration of its scoring prowess and effective passing, Mishawaka crushed visiting Walkerton, 69–34. The Cavemen next hosted Bremen, which "fought a courageous but uphill battle," according to the *South Bend Tribune*, before falling, 41–28. Mishawaka's first road game was at Plymouth, a contest "full of thrills and now and then a touch of football," wrote the *Miskodeed*, in which the visitors prevailed, 45–34. The *Tribune* vividly described Mishawaka's performance with an extended metaphor: "Relentless as a whirlwind, the Maroons of Mishawaka whirled and tossed on the Plymouth reef…and found even the roughest of going not too rough."

The following evening, Mishawaka met defeat at the hands of visiting Fort Wayne Central. The Tigers led 16–6 at halftime, and the Cavemen actually outscored them in the second period but came up short, 35–27. Mishawaka's shooting was off, though, a condition not helped by returning three hours late from Plymouth after the team bus broke down.

Mishawaka returned to its winning ways when Brazil came to town. The visitors were playing their third road game in as many evenings, but they hung with the Cavemen before falling, 43–35. Shelby Shake was unhappy about the quality of his charges' teamwork, as the *Tribune* observed, "Coach Shake was thoroughly disgusted with his team's showing and the mental attitude of its members as well. That something radical is wrong with the Mishawaka squad is apparent, and that something will necessarily have to be ironed out before the squad advances much further into the season."

Alexandria was the Cavemen's next visitor and victim. "The superiority of the Cavemen offense was the deciding factor," observed the *Tribune*. "Coach S.S. Shake's proteges did not attempt anything but a strictly offensive game, peppering the rim from all angles." With a 53–35 triumph, Mishawaka ended a successful December with a 5-1 record.

January began with road wins over Auburn, 44–19, and Valparaiso, 30–24, on consecutive evenings. The team traveled to each contest by train, and the latter game was held in the Valparaiso University gymnasium.

The whole season had been prelude to the highly anticipated showdown with South Bend on January 14. The *Miskodeed* remembered, "Doped to beat South Bend by 20 points, the dope bucket was upset. The Bears started on a rampage and were never headed." In front of five thousand spectators at Notre Dame, Mishawaka fell hard, 35–20. The *Mishawaka Enterprise* offered this explanation of the game's outcome: "Old man 'Overconfidence' knocked at the doors of the Notre Dame gymnasium last night and a quintet of Mishawaka cagers were in the right condition to accept him." Overconfidence was replaced by overreaction as the *Enterprise* reported that "Mishawaka needs a new coach" was heard around town Saturday.

Such talk quickly diminished a few hours later as Shake's men took out their frustration on visiting Nappanee, 60–38. "The ball was in Mishawaka's possession most of the time, so not a great deal of the defensive playing was needed," the *Enterprise* reported.

A week later, the Cavemen defeated Elkhart, 34–23, on the home hardwood but stumbled at Goshen, 43–26. Goshen's hot shooting and Mishawaka's poor defense and faulty teamwork led to the unfavorable result.

The last loss of Mishawaka's regular season came at the hands of the Rochester Zebras. Mishawaka led by one at the half, and the score was 29–29 with three minutes remaining, but the hosts pulled ahead and won, 38–29. The Cavemen's record stood at 9-4 as January ended.

February is the time to get hot in high school basketball, and Mishawaka chose the most opportune game to begin a winning streak. After dropping two straight contests, the Cavemen responded well in the rematch with South Bend, reversing the earlier score and restoring their bragging rights. Mishawaka led the guests, 11–7, at the half, trailed briefly in the second period and then steadily built a lead before employing a stall. The highlight of the game came from Frenchy Denman, who won a tip-off, dribbled into the Bender defense and threw a "backward hook-pass over his head to Doyle" for the layup, wrote the *Enterprise* admiringly. The contest may have had one of the largest crowds ever to witness a game in the old Mishawaka gym. Apparently, the fire marshal had the night off as "an approximate crowd of 3,200 rooters jammed the corners and walls of the gym to see the teams play in the great game. With the additional bleachers, the seating capacity was increased to 2,400, and all of 800 people were standing upstairs and around the court on the playing floor." So full was the gym that some enthusiasts climbed up the outside of the south wall and watched the game through the windows, the bottom of which were about ten feet above the ground. The *Enterprise* included these auditory details: "Representatives of both schools had their own yelling. When both groups were trying to cheer at the same time, the roof seemed to fairly rise from its foundation.

The Mishawaka High school band added to the pep of the local rooters, with its peppy marches."

The wins kept coming. At Bremen, Mishawaka trailed 7–0 but pulled away in the final eight minutes and was victorious, 32–20. The next night, the Cavemen traveled to Kendallville and came home with a solid 49–32 triumph. According to the *Enterprise*, Doyle "proved to be the heart of the Maroon attack." Although he played with a sprained ankle and a "shiner" he received early in the game, Doyle scored five buckets for the Cavemen. Ray DeCook was the leading scorer with 25 points. A week later came the rematch against the visiting Elkhart Blue Blazers, whom Mishawaka humbled again, 39–14. "It was Mishawaka's game from the starting whistle," the *Enterprise* explained. A tougher test came from LaPorte the next day. The visitors had defeated the Cavemen five straight years and led by three at the half, but Mishawaka "came back strong and out-fought and out-played their opponents," wrote the *Miskodeed*, and won, 34–25. The last home game was against Lakeville, which afforded Shake an opportunity to give his second team a workout in the 72–14 drubbing. Led by Doyle's season-high 28 points, "the Maroon offense began rolling down the floor with lightning speed, stopping for nothing," according to the *Enterprise*. Mishawaka finished a perfect February by outlasting Warsaw, 31–27.

The Cavemen ended the regular season with an outstanding 16-4 record that was among the state's top ten in winning percentage. Mishawaka fans were eager for a deep run in the state tourney.

As sectional play began, "the dope" had Mishawaka as the favorite to reclaim the title it had lost so narrowly to South Bend a year earlier. Not only did the Cavemen have the sectional on their court, but the pairings also were advantageous. With ten teams in the local tourney, Mishawaka would play its first-round contest on Friday evening, whereas South Bend would be forced to play three games on Saturday, should they advance to the championship. Mishawaka was hitting its stride in the final weeks of the season, having won seven straight, while South Bend had dropped its last six contests.

The Cavemen were so heavily favored that Mishawaka's greatest foe seemed to be dangerously high overconfidence. According to the *Enterprise*, "Mishawaka rooters are too swell-headed to think of Mishawaka losing. But this is just what will happen if the townspeople do not get down to a little seriousness."

Coach Shake and his team did not seem to have any excessive hubris though. Seared into their memories was the pain of the 1926 sectional. The *Tribune* noted that Shake "is a great believer in the effect of psychology" and was not above intimidating opponents by running up prodigious point totals. Nonetheless, the previous year's sectional defeat had chastened Shake, who would not demand any higher score than was needed to win comfortably. The Mishawaka paper's "Basket Bawls" feature expressed the prudent fan's sentiment when it wrote, "On to the state, Cavemen! But be sure of the sectional first of all."

Mishawaka students were released from school early on Friday, March 4, for the sectional. Before vacating the building, the student body participated in a pep session that morning.

The Mishawaka sectional tipped off at 2:00 p.m. with Lakeville upsetting Madison Township, 19–16, in overtime followed by Hamlet downing Center Township, 30–16.

Mishawaka opened tourney play at 7:30 p.m. in the third contest, matched with Walkerton, which the *Tribune* described as a "scrappy bunch" that might limit the "high geared machine" of Mishawaka's offense. The Cavemen's new uniforms caused a sensation and were perhaps part of Shake's efforts to intimidate opponents. The team's shorts and jerseys had wide vertical stripes with the word *Cavemen* across the chest. One observer suggested the stripes' effect was to make the Mishawakans look "about 7' tall."

The Cavemen overwhelmed Walkerton's defense and took a 20–5 lead into the half. Shake then experimented with Doyle and DeCook as guards and played second-teamers like Toad Doll, Bob Hartzog and Lloyd Butz. Mishawaka nonetheless increased its advantage and cruised to a 39–11 victory, paced by DeCook's 12 points. According to the *Tribune* account, "The athletes with 'the city with the will to do' emblazoned on their suits displayed plenty of will, as well as vim and vigor, in strong arming their opening opponents."

Knox destroyed Grovertown, 70–12, in the fourth game of the opening day.

At nine o'clock Saturday morning, South Bend finally made its tournament debut and defeated North Liberty, 30–11. The next contest went into overtime before Lakeville survived Hamlet, 27–25.

In the first afternoon semifinal, Mishawaka squared off against Knox. Shake used a variety of lineups, including playing DeCook and Doyle as guards, to crush Knox, 41–21.

South Bend defeated Lakeville, 46–13, in the other afternoon game to complete the marquee match-up that everyone in town had hoped for. In hyping the rivals' sectional showdown, "Basket Bawls" implored, "Beat South Bend"; "Annihilate those Bears! Sock 'em hard! Lay 'em low!"; and "Break those Bears into bear bits!" The enmity was not all one-sided though.

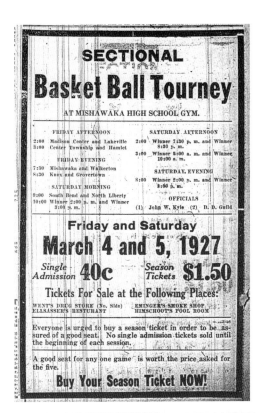

Left: Ads in the *Mishawaka Enterprise* helped bring in huge crowds for the 1927 sectional. *Author's collection.*

Below: The 1927 MHS yearbook showed the team and Coach Shake in the distinctive vertical stripes they wore for the state tourney. *Mishawaka Historical Museum.*

Front Row—Lloyd Butz, Cy Himschoot, Ray De Cook, Al Eminger, Burt Doyle.
Second Row—Jimmy Gosbin, Gordon Weist, Bob Hartzog, Toad Doll.
Third Row—Coach Shake.

Earlier in the week, the *Tribune* had described the "grim determination" shown by the South Bend players in their final practices and suggested that the Bears were capable of upsetting the Cavemen just as they had in the thrilling 1926 sectional finale. Russell Hubbard, a Bender enthusiast, even vowed not to shave until his team defeated Mishawaka in basketball. Mr. Hubbard's whiskers would have many more months to grow.

In front of more than two thousand impassioned fans, the Cavemen gave the Bears their worst beating in the history of the schools' hardwood rivalry. Ray DeCook's layup was the game's first score, and Frenchy Denman followed with a jumper from near the foul line. The Bears got on the board with a free throw. Cy Himschoot's drive netted two more, and DeCook's rebound basket added to Mishawaka's lead. All the Benders could muster in response were 2 more points from the charity stripe. Everything went Mishawaka's way, as evidenced by Denman's mid-court shot hitting nothing but net. After Denman scored again on a layup, Coach Elmer Burnham called time, trailing 14–3 after just nine and a half minutes had ticked away. Mishawaka went into halftime with a commanding 18–6 advantage, and the Bears had yet to score a field goal. "South Bend played a fast floor game but was unable to locate the hoop," the *South Bend News-Times* explained. "The ball was in their possession more than half the initial period but they could not connect with the net."

In the second half, the Mishawaka attack continued unabated, but South Bend did finally pick up its first and only field goal off a Cavemen turnover. It was the exception that proved the rule of just how stifling Mishawaka's zone defense was. The Bears mustered just four points in the second half.

The *Tribune* account of the game noted that Shake "employed a set of formations which completely baffled their opponents" and drew the South Bend guards away from their defensive zone. This enabled DeCook, Denman and Himschoot to "score at ease." On the other end of the court, Himschoot and Eminger played "airtight defense."

When the final horn sounded, Mishawaka had won, 39–10, and captured its second sectional crown in three years. Leading scorers for the Cavemen were DeCook with 11, Himschoot with 10 and Denman with 8.

Mishawaka's sectional title had earned the grudging admiration of the South Bend sportswriters. The *Tribune* used the headline "Bruins Are Outclassed" and offered this praise: "Mishawaka's exhibition was amazing. It is certain that the Maroon-clad cagers reached the heights in basketball perfection.…The ball was handled faultlessly. The Maroons played the delayed offense style with a precision that left South Bend helpless." The

News-Times referred to the Cavemen's performance in the final as "one of the prettiest exhibitions of how basketball should be played that will ever be seen in this section."

Mishawaka High celebrated its sectional victory with an assembly on Monday morning. Postmaster Ralph Gaylor, Coach Shake and team captain Cy Himschoot were the featured speakers. Gaylor congratulated the team and gave special recognition to the seniors. Himschoot urged the student body not to let overconfidence weaken their chances at the regional, and he thanked students and fans for the support they had given the team throughout the season and especially in the sectional championship game. Shake acknowledged South Bend's good sportsmanship, mentioning that Burnham and several Bruin players offered their congratulations and assured him that South Bend would be supporting the Cavemen at the regional and, if they should advance, at the state finals.

After the pep assembly, Mishawaka players and fans began looking ahead in earnest to the regional, which would be held at Notre Dame on March 12. Mishawaka was matched up with New Paris in the opener, followed by Bremen versus Kewanna. New Paris had won the Elkhart sectional after defeating Nappanee in the final, described by the *News-Times* as "one of the greatest upsets in the history of the Elkhart sectional tournament."

The Cavemen were heavily favored to win the school's first regional title. A large banner reading "On to the State" was hung in the entrance hall of the school. The Cavemen's regional chances were solid enough for the *Tribune* to concede, "If Mishawaka hits the mesh Saturday in similar style to their exhibition against South Bend High, a Kansas typhoon won't stop them."

It might not be so easy, the *Enterprise* observed. Although New Paris players were described as "farmer boys" and "corn fed babies," they were rumored to be bigger than Cy Himschoot, including one man who weighed 250 pounds and could "handle the ball like a wizard." Mishawaka held three practices at Notre Dame, gaining familiarity with the court where they would do battle. In a meeting on Wednesday, Shake warned his players that they had not won the regional yet and that anything could happen in thirty minutes of basketball. Simply put, they could not afford to look past New Paris. Instead of "On to the State," the team's motto would have to be "On to New Paris" for the next few days.

In its preview of the regional, the *News-Times* put the spotlight on "a battle of giants" between the opposing centers, Ray DeCook and Pat O'Neill, who were "deadly shots" and each his team's leading scorer.

Comments in the *Enterprise* suggested a mix of both cautious confidence and condescension. While New Paris was described as a small town, the paper repeatedly reminded readers some of their players were over six feet. Fans could not afford to look past "dark horse" New Paris, and Kewanna, favored to defeat Bremen, was a "dangerous" foe that could derail Mishawaka's hopes for state. Such sentiments were prudent, but the *Enterprise* also disparaged New Paris's tiny population of just a few hundred: "New Paris rooters are planning to bring the whole town to the Notre Dame gymnasium for the Saturday afternoon game. If they do, they probably will fill at least the three front rows."

Mishawaka was in a basketball frenzy by Friday evening when hundreds turned out for a community pep rally. Following a "Beat New Paris" banner, students and other fans performed a "snake dance" from the business district at North Main Street and Mishawaka Avenue through downtown to the Hotel Mishawaka on the 200 block of South Main. After many cheers about defeating New Paris and spirited numbers from the band, noted citizens stood on the front steps and addressed the throng of supporters. Frank Steele praised the team and Coach Shake and declared the Cavemen to be unsurpassed statewide in their knowledge of basketball. He added that winning the regional must be the students' first goal, followed by the state finals. Reverend J.A. Burnett of the First Presbyterian Church stated that the town was backing the team and hoping for a regional championship. W.W. French, district governor of the Lions Club, reminded the crowd that student and community support was key to the team's success, and he cautioned against overconfidence. More cheers and music from the band concluded the rally.

The next day, it was time to set aside the hype and actually play the games that everyone had spent the week anticipating. And the Cavemen did not disappoint. In the opener, New Paris proved to be less formidable than some Mishawakans had feared. The Parisians had a narrow lead, 4–3, five minutes into the game until the Cavemen began to wear them down. Two baskets by Ray DeCook put Mishawaka ahead, and they had built a 15–7 advantage by halftime. Shake's strategy in the second half was to augment their lead through a combination of stalling and quick scores. DeCook was the star of the game. Led by his 10 points and 5 from Himschoot, the Cavemen coasted to a 26–15 victory.

Kewanna beat Bremen, 24–19, in the second game to create the expected championship showdown with the Cavemen.

An estimated four thousand fans filled the Notre Dame gymnasium for the title tilt. After five scoreless minutes in which the Cavemen missed several close shots, Cy Himschoot finally put Mishawaka on the board with a free throw, followed shortly by another charity point from DeCook. What came next was dubbed by both the *Enterprise* and the *Tribune* as "the greatest shot in the tournament." Standing at mid-floor, DeCook sent what the *Enterprise* described as a high-arching "beauty through the net. It was so clean that the net did not move over a half an inch in swinging." DeCook's shot gave Mishawaka a 4–0 advantage nine minutes into the game.

The Cavemen then scored at will and built their lead to 16–0 until Kewanna finally got on the board with two minutes left in the half. Mishawaka was in command, 19–2, at the intermission.

Mishawaka continued to dominate in the second half, running the score up to 28–2 while Kewanna was struggling for another field goal. Shake felt confident enough at this point that he pulled his starters, who left the court to a rousing cheer from the Cavemen faithful. Kewanna took advantage of the substitute five and scored four more baskets. Kewanna may have wished there was a mercy rule in high school basketball, but the final buzzer eventually ended their suffering. The Cavemen were triumphant, 38–15, and took home the regional championship. Mishawaka had punched its ticket for the state finals.

Doyle and DeCook led the Cavemen with twelve points apiece; Denman added nine. The *News-Times* explained that most of Doyle's six field goals came from under the basket after he had weaved his way through the Kewanna defense. DeCook's five baskets were "from every angle and from every part of the floor." "The entire Mishawaka team played a great game," assessed the *News-Times*. "They failed to show much on defense, but this was largely because their offense was their best defense. They got and held possession of the ball and Kewanna couldn't do much scoring while that condition persisted.…The superiority of the Cavemen was never in doubt."

Under the tourney format used by the IHSAA at the time, winners of the sixteen regionals advanced to the state finals, held March 18–19 at the Exposition Building on the Indiana State Fairgrounds in Indianapolis. Then, as now, the enormous structure was used for the cattle display at the state fair, earning it the nickname of the "Cow Barn." Throughout their tournament run, Mishawaka fans had thought in terms of winning one of sixteen "stalls" in the Cow Barn as a metaphor for qualifying for the state finals. "Basket Bawls" could now proudly crow, "On to the Cow Barn!"

When the Cavemen got to Indianapolis, they would be matched with the Gary Emerson Norsemen, also known as the "Golden Tornado," in the seventh opening round game, scheduled for 7:30 p.m. on Friday. For the first time in the tournament, Mishawaka was not the obvious favorite and was an underdog in the eyes of many. Emerson had eliminated Froebel, the last undefeated team in the state, and had a tougher schedule than the Cavemen's, including more difficult opposition in the sectional and regional. The *Gary Post-Tribune* reported that Ralph Brasaemle, Emerson's coach, expected a "hard-fought battle with the powerful Mishawaka offense a constant threat against the Norse defenses that bulked so strong" in earlier rounds of the tourney. "Watch those Maroons. They are nothing more or less than dangerous," the *Post-Tribune* warned.

The South Bend papers and many other downstate "dopesters" favored the Norsemen, and the *Enterprise* had to convince its readers—and perhaps the team—that Mishawaka had a chance. Its commentary alternated between acknowledging concern and building optimism: "Emerson will prove a hard team to conquer and the Maroons will be very fortunate if they pass the 'Golden Tornado.' On the whole matters look quite dark for the Maroons, but if they keep plenty of confidence in themselves, they may spring the surprise of a real 'dark horse' team. Then wouldn't the town of Mishawaka go wild!" The *Enterprise* also suggested that if Mishawaka brought enough fans to Indianapolis "the Maroons should be able to win their game with noise." The "Basket Bawls" column added, "Take a little of the steel out of Gary"; "Sock it to 'em, Cavemen!"; and "Mishawaka can, Mishawaka will!"

Seeking more evidence to ascertain the Norsemen's chances, the *Post-Tribune* offered a detailed study of Emerson and Mishawaka's offenses, defenses and performances against common opponents. They found Mishawaka better offensively and Emerson stronger defensively. Both schools had defeated Valparaiso, LaPorte and South Bend, although Mishawaka had also lost once to the Benders. Emerson had beaten Fort Wayne Central, but Mishawaka had fallen to them at home. The Cavemen had one fewer loss, yet Emerson's defeats had come at the hands of stronger teams. In sum, the analysis of the scores and opponents "reveals no adequate reason why the Norsemen shouldn't triumph over the Maroons."

On the Wednesday before state, Mishawaka's ten players were given physicals required by the IHSAA. Then, at the invitation of Notre Dame's Coach Keogan, they practiced at the Notre Dame gym. The fifty-by-seventy-six-foot court and backboards at Notre Dame were the same as what the Cavemen would see at the Cow Barn, which Mishawaka hoped would give them a slight advantage over the Norsemen. In the practice at Notre Dame, the Cavemen held a shooting session followed by a vigorous twenty-minute scrimmage.

Coach Shake urged his charges not to think of any other games or teams besides Emerson. Earlier, though, Shake himself had violated this admonition by telling the *Enterprise* that he really wanted a crack at Logansport, one of the state's top teams.

In the days before state, concern arose over the health of Cy Himschoot, who had developed a cold during the New Paris game. Himschoot's cough had been so bad that he nearly was withdrawn from the game. To facilitate Himschoot's recovery, Shake did not scrimmage the team at Tuesday's practice. Fortunately, Himschoot had improved by the Wednesday practice at Notre Dame.

To the cheers of the student body, Mishawaka left for the state finals at 1:00 p.m. on Thursday, traveling by charter bus. Shake planned to have his team watch several of the games on Friday prior to their clash with Emerson, hoping that they may get to see future opponents. Meanwhile, the Norsemen had traveled to the Circle City by train.

Everyone in the state seemed to have an opinion about who would win the tourney. Two of the favorites were Logansport and Martinsville, but the draw had them pitted against each other in the last contest of the first round. In essence, their game might be for the state championship. Logansport, the majority's pick to win it all, had lost only one game, and Martinsville had three losses. Making its fifth straight appearance in the state finals, Martinsville had won the state championship in 1924 and was state runner-up in 1926. Logansport had earned its third trip to the finals in four seasons. Muncie and Bedford were the strongest contenders from the upper bracket. Muncie had only lost to Martinsville, and Bedford had defeated Martinsville twice.

Few gave Mishawaka much chance of winning the whole tournament, and the Indianapolis papers picked Mishawaka to lose in the first round. At least publicly, Coach Shake claimed not to mind such low expectations. "This is the best place in the world for us to be," he said prior to the team's departure for Indianapolis. "We want to be the underdog so that if we lose nothing much will be thought of us, but if we win, we can be called a 'dark horse' team."

The lack of respect given to Mishawaka may have resulted from being one of the three newcomers to the finals and its relatively easy path through the sectional and regional. Nonetheless, the Cavemen had averaged an impressive 40 points per game (1,002 points) on the season. The *Tribune* reported that the Cavemen were "determined to give their opponents the fight of their lives and at least to eliminate some of the favorites from the tourney." The *Enterprise* tried to stay hopeful: "It would not surprise many Mishawaka fans if the Maroons would prove the 'dark horse' of the tournament and win the state finals. Such is luck."

During the week, the *Enterprise* encouraged readers to come to Indianapolis to support the Cavemen. Most who made the trip did so by car down the Dixie Highway, but others traveled by train or interurban, taking advantage of special reduced fares for the state finals. Those back in Mishawaka could listen to WSBT radio's play-by-play returns or call a special phone number the *Enterprise* had set up to get the latest score from the Cow Barn. Similar arrangements had been made for the Gary faithful. A "leased wire" would connect the *Post-Tribune* sports editor at the game with a "fan party" held in the Gary YMCA's gymnasium, where a representative of the paper would "megaphone" the updates to the anxious fans.

Indianapolis was expecting the largest crowd yet for a basketball state finals. A few days before the finals, two thousand fans waiting to buy tickets had been turned away from the Exposition Building when the IHSAA announced that the last ticket had been sold. "The entire city had caught the basketball spirit," the *Post-Tribune* described. "Gayly costumed rooters with bands and drum corps and other picturesque arrivals were expected."

Built in 1924, the Exposition Building was hosting its third state finals. The building's capacity for basketball was 12,500 spectators, seated on temporary pine bleachers built for the event. The Cow Barn's interior and exterior appearances are largely unchanged today, which makes it easy for a visitor to the Indiana State Fair to stroll through the building and imagine what the Cavemen would have seen in 1927. Measuring 731 feet by 234 feet, the Cow Barn's interior is a vast open space uninterrupted by posts or dividers. Its ceiling of exposed metal girders is about the height of a typical high school gym, and large windows run the length of the building on both the main level and just below the ceiling. For day games, the interior would have been suffused with natural light.

Bedford and Evansville Central kicked off the festivities at 9:00 a.m. As the day progressed, the Cow Barn and its surroundings were a scene appropriate for the state fairgrounds. The *News* described the spectacle: "Large delegations from all towns whose teams are represented, were on hand, several with groups numbering in the hundreds and a few passing the 1,000 mark. All had yell leaders who were prominent individuals in the intervals between games. The police found it hard to keep the aisles cleared of fans who were more intent on basketball than fire regulations."

Finally, it was time for Mishawaka and Emerson to take their place on high school basketball's grandest stage. The Cavemen's striped uniforms caused

The Exposition Building (also known as the "Cow Barn") at the Indiana State Fairgrounds was the site of the 1927 state finals. *IHSAA.*

a stir in the crowd and led the *News* to refer to Shake's men as "the not too mildly clad court performers." The *Post-Tribune* described the attire as "the flashiest seen on the tournament floor—pink and white stripes throughout."

Mishawaka and Emerson each had at least 300 fans in attendance. The Emerson crowd was in a corner, and the Cavemen faithful "were a tiny knot of rooters on the sidelines," according to the *News-Times*. Despite their small number, "They made their presence decisively felt. The great auditorium was dominated by their shrill 'Fight 'em, Cavemen,' which made itself heard through the din." Emerson fans countered with a "Beat Mishawaka!" chant. The teams played in front of a packed house because the featured bout on the evening card was the final game, pitting Logansport and Martinsville. Estimates suggested that Logansport had brought a finals-record crowd of between 1,500 and 2,000 rooters.

Emerson drew first blood by scoring on free throws after two Cavemen fouls. Ray DeCook's short basket tied the game. Emerson immediately retook the lead when Burnam evaded the defenders and put in a field goal. Mishawaka matched them with DeCook's bomb from mid-floor. After a basket by Burt Doyle, Emerson's Wood quickly responded with a layup. A deft pass to Wood, who slashed his way in for another score, made Shake call time, trailing 8–6.

After the timeout, DeCook scored another field goal and, seconds later, a free throw to reclaim the lead for the Cavemen. Cy Himschoot hit a charity shot and then, according to the *Tribune*, "looped one two-thirds the length of the floor." Mishawaka went into halftime with a 12–8 advantage. To their fans' jubilation, the Cavemen were just fifteen minutes away from advancing to the final eight of the state tourney.

Opening the second half, Doyle's free throw added to Mishawaka's lead, but Emerson responded with a pair of Burnam buckets. After several missed opportunities by both teams, Emerson took the lead, 14–13, with a field goal by Stanford from mid-court. Just seconds later, Wood scored again, followed by Burnam's long one. In just two minutes of play, the Norsemen had surged to a commanding 5-point lead, which compelled Shake to call timeout again. He knew that the game was slipping away.

"Dazed by the sudden turn of events, Mishawaka discarded its passing attack and bombarded the basket from far out on the floor in an unsuccessful effort to regain the lead, while its opponents continued their accurate net-sniping and increased the advantage point by point," wrote the *Indianapolis Star*.

The *News-Times* offered this account of the second half's turn of events: "Emerson's defense began to function in its wonted style and the shots secured by the Cavemen were few and far between. The wearers of the Maroon strove courageously to break through, but their efforts were nullified by the pernicious activities of 'Red' Burnam, who could not be stopped. From under the basket, from the side, from far back on the floor, the big Gary forward dropped them in. Apparently he could not miss."

Emerson added to their advantage when Burnam scored from beneath the basket, but Bob Hartzog responded for the Cavemen with a tip-in and then a free throw. After Himschoot and DeCook each missed long attempts, Stanford got free and hit a "sucker shot" for Gary to make the score 22–16. DeCook got a tip-in, but the Norsemen replied with two more Burnam field goals. DeCook made a free throw after Attenhof's foul. Mishawaka's final points came on DeCook's long toss from half-court, but Emerson had the last word when Attenhof put in a field goal from the same distance just before the final buzzer sounded.

Emerson was victorious, 28–21, and Mishawaka's season came to an unhappy end. In a tale of two contrasting halves, the Cavemen could not survive being outscored 20–9 in the second half. The *Post-Tribune* was impressed that Emerson needed only a few minutes to erase Mishawaka's 5-point lead, a margin that "bulked mighty large in the tournament with its 15-minute halves." The teams had played evenly in the final few minutes, but it was too late and not enough for Mishawaka.

DeCook was outstanding for the Cavemen, netting twelve points. Doyle, Hartzog and Himschoot added three apiece. Mishawaka, though, simply had no solution for Burnam, who led all scorers with fifteen points. "When Burnam started hitting the hoop, the result was never in doubt," explained the *News-Times*, "although the Cavemen fought courageously until the final gun sounded the death knell of their hopes….Al Eminger and DeCook covered themselves with glory in the battle with Emerson." DeCook was given honorable mention on the *Indianapolis News*'s all-state team, but Jim Gallagher of the *News-Times* felt that DeCook "played brilliantly" and deserved third-team status.

Emerson was able to enjoy its conquest for less than a day. Led by junior Johnny Wooden, who was Shelby Shake's second cousin, Martinsville advanced to the round of eight after embarrassing Logansport and its legion of fans, 27–14. The Artesians then dispatched the Norsemen, 26–14, in the quarterfinals and Connersville, 32–21, to reach the state championship game. Martinsville outlasted Muncie, 26–23, to win the school's second state title.

The *Enterprise* voiced its disappointment over the Cavemen's state finals performance: "Mishawaka made a very poor showing against the Emerson quintet.…They cracked at the stalling game in the second part of the game…when Emerson got the lucky shooting streak." The paper did try to accentuate the season's positives by adding, "But, Mishawaka was one of the first 16 teams out of 733 in Indiana, and this is quite an honor."

Gallagher offered his postmortem on Mishawaka's performance: "Mishawaka and South Bend have no reason to be ashamed at the showing of Mishawaka's Cavemen. While the Norsemen crept away from them in the second half, and they were unable to pierce the Emerson defense, they kept on battling courageously. They seemed perhaps a trifle stage-struck, and they had few friends in the vast crowd, but they played a hard game, and a clean game, and none of their few followers were ashamed of their allegiance after the game."

Even in defeat, life—and athletics—went on at Mishawaka High. The *Enterprise* noted that spring sports were already underway. Several of the basketball players were participants, and Coaches Steele and Shake would soon be focusing on the football and track teams. Shake, though, "will probably take a short rest after the strenuous basketball season."

Under Shelby Shake's mentorship, Mishawaka basketball teams would continue their greatest era of success. In addition to the sectional titles of 1925 and 1927, the Cavemen repeated in 1928 and were victorious again in 1935 and 1937. Never again, though, would any of Shake's teams advance beyond the regional. In eleven years at the Mishawaka helm, Shake posted a record of 141-114 and had eight winning seasons, both still school records.

Mishawaka won a sectional in 1939 under Raymond "Dutch" Struck, but it was not until 1955 that the Cavemen exceeded the achievements of 1927. After winning the sectional and regional, Coach John Longfellow's team made the championship game of the semi-state before falling to Fort Wayne North. The 1955 "elite eight" finish remains the farthest any Mishawaka basketball team—boys or girls—has advanced in the state tourney. The Cavemen reached the regional championship game in both 1975 and 1986, but the years since have seen the most prolonged drought of postseason boys' basketball success in school history. Those halcyon days of 1927 and 1955 seem far away indeed.

A January 1937 post-game altercation between Coach Shake and Johnny Wooden, then coach at South Bend Central, later led the IHSAA to force Mishawaka to relieve Shake of his coaching duties. Shake resigned, left Mishawaka and taught at Southern Illinois University. He never coached again.

Cy Himschoot and Ray DeCook were among the Mishawaka High School Athletic Hall of Fame's inaugural inductees in 1986. Shelby Shake joined them in 1999.

The Cavemen's great basketball season of 1926–27 soon passed into memory. As the decades went by, it was all but forgotten by the community. The boys who led Mishawaka to glory and the state finals grew to maturity, became old men and are now all long gone.

Of the remarkable events Mishawakans experienced in 1927, playing in the state finals may seem the most mundane, but it has also proven to be the most difficult to duplicate. Lindbergh's solo flight across the Atlantic has been repeated on countless occasions, Ruth's single-season home run record has been surpassed seven times, but the Mishawaka Cavemen are still waiting for a return trip to the basketball state finals.

MISHAWAKA'S BATTLEGROUND

Celebrating the Eightieth Anniversary of Steele Stadium's WPA Bleachers

B oston has Bunker Hill. San Antonio has the Alamo. Quebec City has the Plains of Abraham.

Unlike these cities, Mishawaka has never had armies fight within its borders, but it does have an ancient battleground, where young men have prepared for war and struggled against opponents. This place is the most contested piece of ground in the Princess City: Mishawaka High School's football field, known today as Steele Stadium.

When surging enrollment growth in the early 1920s forced School City of Mishawaka to replace the overcrowded high school building at 402 Lincolnway West, Superintendent P.C. Emmons selected a site on the north side of the 1200 block of Lincolnway East. The new Mishawaka High opened in the fall of 1924, a magnificent edifice that provided a state-of-the-art facility to accommodate the educational needs of the city's booming population.

The campus plan for the new high school included a football field north of the building on land bounded by Gernhart Avenue, Linden Avenue and Studebaker Street. According to the 1946 *Miskodeed* yearbook, soil was brought from the Mishawaka Hills to fill in the land that became the gridiron where generations of Mishawakans would play and watch football. The Cavemen played their first game there on September 18, 1926.

In its early years, the facility was known simply as School Field and included a cinder track encircling the football field. Wooden bleachers stood west of the field, beyond the track. Home games were played on Saturday afternoons until lights were installed in 1937, beginning the tradition of Friday night football in Mishawaka.

Mishawaka High's football team had won a mythical state championship in 1920, but the program came into its golden age after Frank Steele became head coach in 1924. Football became the school's most successful sport and its greatest claim to fame. The Cavemen, also known as the Maroons, were a perennial power in the Northern Indiana High School Conference, and Steele's teams claimed mythical state championships in 1925 and 1926. Russell Arndt became head coach in 1933 and led the Cavemen to another state championship in 1935.

The success of the football program and continued growth of the student body prompted school officials to consider ways to improve Mishawaka High's campus and facilities. To do so, they turned to the Works Progress Administration (WPA), a federal work-relief program. The WPA used federal funds to cover labor costs, providing temporary, part-time jobs that pumped money into the economy and improved the hopes, self-esteem and job skills of the unemployed. Local governments covered the cost of materials, such as brick, stone and concrete.

On February 22, 1938, Emmons announced plans to partner with the WPA to build bleachers made of reinforced concrete and brick for Mishawaka High's football field. Engineer Charles Cole of South Bend was hired to make the designs, which would be similar to a stadium in Fort Smith, Arkansas. Early estimates were for an $80,000 project, of which School City would pay $30,000 to $40,000. The WPA would cover 60 percent of the total cost, all common labor expenses, as much of the skilled labor as possible and part of the expense of materials.

Initial plans called for construction of stands on the west side of the field only. They would be approximately three hundred feet long and fifty feet wide at the base. Beneath the bleachers would be five classrooms to relieve overcrowding in the vocational department, dressing rooms and showers, storage room for band equipment, public restrooms and concession stands.

On February 26, the school board approved a resolution of intent to issue bonds for $40,000 to cover its share of the project. When the bonds were advertised in the *Mishawaka Enterprise* on March 3, the project description included concrete-and-brick construction, a seating capacity of more than four thousand persons, between six and eight classrooms, locker rooms, office and shower rooms and heating and plumbing equipment.

To dissuade opposition to the bond issue, Superintendent Emmons continually shared with the media new details about the stadium. The March

10 issue of the *Tribune* included a sketch of an aerial view of the bleachers. Three days later, the paper reported that Emmons had approved the revised design, which now called for 4,200 seats, a press box, restrooms, two concession stands, four rooms for "school purposes" such as classrooms and locker rooms and showers for 130 boys. The article also provided specifics about the economic boon the project would provide. Cole estimated that the cost for materials to be purchased locally would be $39,055. Of that sum, the WPA would provide $7,000, and School City would spend $32,055. About two hundred men would be needed for several months of construction, and businesses would supply sand and gravel, cement, reinforcing steel, brick, mortar, windows and doors, structural iron and pipe, wood seats, heating, plumbing, electrical, construction equipment and engineering services.

Fearful of falling behind Mishawaka in the area high school football arms race, the South Bend School Board announced on March 28 its tentative plans for the WPA to construct concrete bleachers on the north side of its own School Field. The 5,800-seat stands would increase the stadium's capacity to more than 12,000 spectators. Existing wooden bleachers on the south side of the field would remain, and the wooden stands that had been on the north side would be moved behind each end zone. The new bleachers were ready for use in September.

On April 8, plans for Mishawaka's WPA bleachers came to a screeching halt when the school board was informed by attorneys representing bond buyers that it had no authority to issue bonds for facilities that were to be used solely for athletics. P.C. Emmons acknowledged that classrooms beneath the stands were still being contemplated, but their likelihood had diminished; as a result, the school board had reclassified the project as exclusively for athletic use.

Despite this setback, Superintendent Emmons and School City had not given up on the dream of constructing a first-class football stadium, and by early June they were pursuing Plan B. Instead of the original $80,000 price tag, the project was scaled back to $60,000. A WPA labor grant for $46,240 would cover the bulk of expenses. Penn Township would become a project sponsor by providing $9,000 worth of materials, and the school board and high school's athletic board of control would offer $8,000. No bonding would be needed to cover the school system's expenses because existing funds could be shifted from one maintenance and facilities account to another.

The June 7 issue of the *Tribune* that announced these plans also included other details about the stadium project. The bleachers would be three hundred feet long, extending from goal line to goal line; forty-four feet wide; and twenty-one rows high. Because the new stands would not be completed before the 1938 football season began, the existing wooden bleachers would be moved to the east side of the field for use that fall.

A July 12 public hearing on the project offered no significant opposition, and William Jordan, district director of the WPA, announced on July 23 that President Franklin Roosevelt had approved $58,895 for the Mishawaka High concrete bleachers project. As per its final agreement with the WPA, School City would be responsible for providing $11,410 to help fund the project, which Jordan stated would employ 133 men for 420 working days.

After months of proposals, meetings and revisions, construction of the bleachers finally began on August 10 as a dozen WPA workers placed stakes and began digging at the worksite. "Almost overnight a timekeeper's shack, a tool house and W.P.A. workmen appeared," wrote the 1939 *Miskodeed*, "and mammoth holes were dug where the old wooden bleachers had formerly stood."

On September 23, the school board approved $4,300 in expenditures for materials and equipment used for the west bleachers. Among these were thirty thousand feet of rough lumber purchased at a price of $1,000, special metal seat frames for $500 and $1,843 worth of reinforcing steel and wire mesh.

Beginning at the north end, forms were set up for the first of six sections before the end of September, and concrete was poured during the second week of October. Because of favorable weather in October and November, crews were able to form and pour a section per week, resulting in the bleachers' rapid progress southward toward the high school building. Fans attending home games that fall could now easily envision the stands where they would be cheering in a year's time.

The October 14 *Tribune* reported that work crews had varied between fifty and one hundred men. That article also noted that the basic construction of the bleachers might be completed by the November 11 season finale against Riley, but they would only be used "in case of emergency" because the seats would not yet have been installed. By November 18, the stands were nearly complete, and construction of the forty-eight-foot-long press box began that day. On November 27, a shipment of ten thousand board feet of California redwood arrived at R.J. Corlett & Sons lumberyard and, after being treated, was to be installed for the stadium's seating.

Concrete in the south end of the bleachers was barely dry when Mishawaka school officials made public on November 18 the exciting news

West bleachers under construction, 1938. *Mishawaka Historical Museum.*

that the WPA would also build bleachers on the east side of the field. The stands would cost $70,305, but School City, as sponsor, would again bear only a fraction of that sum. The federal government would provide $58,895, and the school system would contribute $11,400. The athletic board of control would offer $1,000 to defray some of that expense, and Penn Township pledged $7 per man per month for labor, which was expected to total approximately $2,000. As a result, School City's actual share of the project was reduced to $8,000.

The east stands were similar but not identical to the west bleachers. Also built of reinforced concrete and brick, the east bleachers would have a seating capacity of 3,800 persons. They would extend end zone to end zone—making the east bleachers actually twenty yards longer than their western counterpart—in eight sections and be four rows shorter. The structure's height was limited by the space available between the track and the rear of the bleachers, which immediately abutted the sidewalk along the west side of Gernhart. The proposal called for the east stands to be completed before the first home game, ensuring that Mishawaka would begin the 1939 campaign in what the *Tribune* predicted would be "one of the finest prep football stadiums in the state."

On February 16, 1939, Mishawaka school officials received word that the WPA in Washington, D.C., had formally approved the stadium project. This would cover funding the east bleachers and the finishing touches on the interior of the west stands, including the shower and dressing rooms, restrooms, storage rooms and concession stands. On March 28, President Roosevelt authorized $58,790 for the federal government's share of the remaining work at School Field. The WPA designated workers for the project in early and mid-April, and construction began on April 26.

The Mishawaka Lions Club toured the new football stadium on May 4. P.C. Emmons hosted a luncheon for the group in the school cafeteria, and Charles Bingham, secretary of the school board, also spoke to the Lions. In his report on the stadium project, Emmons summarized the expenditures to date, which included sponsor's costs of $13,643 for the west bleachers. The board of control contributed $1,100 of this amount, and Penn Township added $3,930. He also explained that the sponsor's share for the east bleachers would be $9,640, which would be covered by $3,000 from the board of control, $3,000 from Penn Township and $3,640 from School City. The Lions were told that construction officials and engineers were referring to the stadium as one of the best high school football facilities in the Midwest. Athletic director Frank Steele joined the tour and explained that the finished stadium would have a seating capacity of 8,000 and that temporary bleachers in the end zones could add another 1,500.

While the WPA workers were hurrying to complete the east bleachers in August, Coach Russell Arndt and his assistants, Walter "Dutch" Thurston and Raymond "Dutch" Struck, were just beginning their own construction project, making sure that the 1939 Maroons would be worthy of the stadium in which they played.

Arndt and his men were actually engaged in more of a *rebuilding* effort. The 1938 edition of the Cavemen had posted a 7-3 record and defeated the three South Bend high schools (Central, Washington and Riley) to win the *Tribune* Shield, awarded by the *South Bend Tribune* for the Inter-City Championship. Mishawaka's 14–6 victory over archrival South Bend Central at Notre Dame Stadium gave the Maroons their first Hickory Stick since 1935. Fourteen lettermen graduated the following June, though, leaving the coaching staff to work with "only a skeleton of that fine team," in the *Tribune*'s words, as sixty players began camp at Merrifield Park in mid-August. Captain Joe Gall, All-Conference and Inter City center, was the lone returning regular starter. Of the boys vying for the other starting positions, none had played in more than two or three contests the previous season.

Mr. Thurston, Mr. Arndt, Mr. Struck, Mr. Steele (in circle).

Cavemen on the Gridiron

The 1940 *Miskodeed* included photos of the football coaches and Athletic Director Frank Steele. *Mishawaka Historical Museum.*

Coach Arndt acknowledged the situation by stating, "The present squad is one of the most inexperienced Mishawaka has had for several years."

The young Maroons would face baptism by fire in their home opener on September 8 against Mooseheart (Illinois) Academy. Founded in 1913 as a home for the widows and children of members of the Loyal Order of Moose, Mooseheart Academy soon became known for its football team, which was so dominant that local teams refused to schedule it. As a result, Mooseheart traveled around the Midwest and throughout the country to play a formidable list of opponents, leading to their nickname: the "Red Ramblers." In the previous twenty-two seasons, Mooseheart had posted a combined record of 133-36-11 and had never had a losing season. The Red Ramblers returned a roster that was largely intact from the team that went 5-3-1 in 1938, and they had been practicing since August 1.

The Cavemen were an underdog heading into the opener, which prompted Arndt to intensify their practice regimen. Along with the usual two-a-day

Top Row: Cobb, Trittipo, Moore, Shaffer, Baiz, Thompson, Scheibelhut, Kline, Linson, Koontz.
Third Row: Fansler, Stuart, Pozwilka, Smith, Richardson, DeVreese, Wachs, Stockberger, Carnes, Good, Savage.
Second Row: Rupchock, Muninch, Williams, Van Durman, Katterheinrich, Gall, Sanders, Steele, Kopsea, Van de Putte, Hoffman.
First Row: DeVolder, Houghton, Maggioli, J. Deal, Ballatore, L. Deal, Severa, Heftie, Herron, La Vine, Savage.

The 1939 Mishawaka High School football team. *Mishawaka Historical Museum.*

workouts, he held several offensive scrimmages during the last week of August and a four-quarter "secret scrimmage under game conditions," according to the *Tribune*, to test both offense and defense on Saturday, September 2. The following Tuesday, Mishawaka went under the lights at the new stadium for another "secret drill."

A record crowd was anticipated for the Mooseheart game. The new stands, the first contest of the season and a tough opponent would draw several thousand fans. Moose lodges in the area had been selling advance tickets, eager to give "moral support" and "to see their wards uphold the name of their lodge," stated the *Enterprise*. More than one thousand Mooseheart supporters were expected to make the trip from Illinois. Although it was the inaugural event for the WPA-built bleachers, the stadium's formal dedication was scheduled for the final game of the year, the November 10 clash with Riley.

Mishawakans spent the first week of September eagerly anticipating the debut of their new stadium and the start of the season. Their thoughts were not entirely about football, though. On September 1, Germany unleashed its *blitzkrieg* against neighboring Poland, beginning a world war that would eventually affect the lives of everyone in the stands and on the field that

Friday night. Days after the onslaught began, Great Britain and France declared war against Germany, and Americans began to worry about their country being pulled into the conflict. The same newspapers whose sports pages previewed the first week of local gridiron battles also carried ominous headlines and articles about Europe once again spiraling into self-destruction. As Mishawaka anxiously followed the war news, Friday's game took on the added value of being a temporary distraction from more serious and disturbing ruminations.

Game conditions were ideal—sixty-three degrees and fair skies—as the teams took the field for the 8:00 p.m. kickoff; 4,500 fans were present to witness the historic contest.

If the rooters for both schools came to see offensive prowess, they were soon disappointed. Mishawaka and Mooseheart played scoreless ball in the first quarter, "displaying a complete lack of power," in the words of the *Tribune*'s Wendell Jollief. In the second stanza, the Red Ramblers' quick kick was blocked by the Maroons, who recovered the ball on their own 45. Bob Wachs's throw to Larry Deal resulted in a 25-yard gain, but the drive stalled after two incompletions and a running play. The Cavemen stymied the Red Ramblers on their next possession. Bob Herron received Mooseheart's punt on the Mishawaka 40 and took it to the Red Ramblers' 47. After a few running plays had negative yardage, Harry Heftie's pass to Dick Steele resulted in a 30-yard gain, putting the ball on the Mooseheart 30. The Cavemen gained 3 more yards on a pass but could get no closer to the end zone, and the Red Ramblers took over on downs. Charley Rider, their star fullback, scampered for 33 yards, the longest gain by either team, but Mooseheart failed to convert the drive into points. When halftime paused hostilities, the combatants went under the west bleachers in a scoreless tie.

In the second half, Mishawaka was plagued by an offense that went nowhere, and Mooseheart spent most of the half in Cavemen territory. The Maroons' defense often bent but did not break, keeping the Red Ramblers away from pay dirt. The most dramatic play of the game came partway through the fourth quarter when Delbert Dixon, the Mooseheart quarterback, threw to Rider, who caught the ball but stepped out of bounds at the back of the end zone. Neither team was able to score, and the game ended in an unusual 0–0 tie.

The *Tribune* account asserted that Mishawaka fans felt they had won a "moral victory" over the favored Red Ramblers, and the *Enterprise* called it "a great showing." The Cavemen's ground attack had been nearly nonexistent, netting just 13 yards and not a single first down. The aerial campaign had been better: 3 for 18, good for 61 yards and all three Mishawaka first downs. Mooseheart had figured out the Mishawaka passing game by the end of the first half, though, and denied the hosts any success in the second half.

The following week, Mishawaka hosted the Gary Tolleston Blue Raiders. Coach Arndt made several lineup changes, including starting Achille "Chick" Maggioli at fullback and Heftie at quarterback. The game was ultimately decided on a series of plays at the end of the first quarter and the start of the second. Maggioli fumbled on the Cavemen 8-yard line and then attempted to quickly punt the ball even though it was only third down. Six Tolleston players piled on top of him and recovered the pigskin on the 6 to end the quarter. Two runs later, the Blue Raiders were in the end zone with what proved to be the game's only score. Mishawaka outperformed their guests in passing and total yards but again failed to put together a scoring drive and lost, 6–0. The home crowd was left wondering when the new School Field bleachers would see their first Cavemen points.

The next two weeks, Mishawaka took to the road against Fort Wayne North and South Bend Washington. Against the Redskins, the Maroons finally generated some offense but could not contain North's passing attack and dropped the contest, 25–14. Washington, who would go on to win the conference title, completely outclassed the visitors, 20–0, in front of twelve thousand fans at School Field. The *Miskodeed* later praised Mishawaka's "fighting spirit" but noted that the Panthers' "machine-like precision" and "savage blocking and tackling" were too much for the Cavemen.

Mishawaka returned home the following week and finally scored against Goshen. In the second quarter, Heftie's 53-yard touchdown run gave the Maroons a lead they would not relinquish. Mishawaka's second score came late in the third quarter, set up by Heftie intercepting a pass on the Redskins' 37-yard line. Five plays later, Deal "carried the mail in fancy style," in the *Tribune*'s words, as he pounded through the center of the line for a 10-yard gain and crossed the goal line still standing. Arndt's team finished triumphant, 12–0.

The biggest victory of the season came a week later when the Cavemen upset the visiting Elkhart Blue Blazers, who had won thirteen consecutive conference games. As a crowd of seven thousand watched, Elkhart fumbled on the first play from scrimmage, and Mishawaka recovered on the Elkhart 26. With the ball on the 9, Deal veered off the left tackle and through the Blazers' line for the score. Mishawaka contained Elkhart's offense the rest of the game, including thwarting a third-quarter drive that reached the Cavemen's 8, and secured the win, 6–0.

Just when the Maroons were showing signs of being a solid team, they dropped the next two contests. Along the shore of Lake Maxinkuckee, the Culver Military Academy Cadets scored a touchdown in the second stanza and two more in the third, including a 30-yard interception return. Rex Shaffer's 1-yard run capped off an 83-yard Cavemen drive in the fourth quarter, but it was too little, too late to prevent the 18–7 defeat. Twenty thousand watched the annual clash with South Bend Central at Notre Dame Stadium. The "swift charging and deadly tackling" of the Mishawaka defense, led by Lloyd Katerheinrich and Charles Rupchock, limited the Bears' running attack to just 58 yards. Central managed to turn their opportunities into two touchdowns, though, and held the Cavemen scoreless. "Outscored, but not outplayed or outfought," wrote the *Miskodeed*, "the valiant Maroons lost to their alert Bear rivals, 13–0."

Mishawaka next hosted the Clinton Wildcats. Harry Heftie's 3-yard touchdown pass to Steele put the Maroons ahead in the second quarter. When Clinton tied the game in the third quarter, the Cavemen responded with "swiftness and ferocity," the yearbook recalled, in the fourth frame as Heftie handed off a reverse to Shaffer, who took it in for the 5-yard score. Mishawaka won, 14–7.

The Maroons' season came to a climax on November 10 against Riley. This game was also Homecoming and included an impressive pregame dedication of the new stadium. The Wildcats, 5-4, had beaten Central the previous week and entered the contest as a slight favorite.

Mishawaka school officials went all out to give their new stadium a fitting ceremony that began at 7:30 p.m.; 6,500 people endured blasts of wind and thirty-seven-degree weather to watch as fireworks spelled out "Dedicating M.H.S. Stadium" to start the event. Alumni who were football lettermen, dating all the way back to the school's first team in 1898, had been invited to participate in the festivities. After gathering in the school cafeteria "to recall memories of victories of yesteryear," according to the *Tribune*, the 150 former athletes paraded into the stadium, led by Mishawaka's marching band, and sat in a special reserved section near midfield of the west bleachers. Next, the American flag was raised near the south end zone, and the Mishawaka and Riley bands together played "The Star-Spangled Banner."

At 7:45 p.m., Superintendent Emmons spoke, followed by A.P. Crabtree, the state WPA educational supervisor, who formally handed over Mishawaka High School Stadium on behalf of the WPA. Charles Bingham, now school board president, gave a brief speech of acceptance, and a letter of greetings from Arthur Trester, commissioner of the Indiana High School

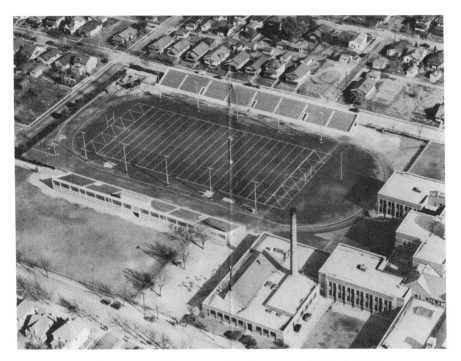

This aerial view of the new stadium appeared in the program for the dedication ceremony. *Mishawaka Historical Museum.*

Athletic Association, was read. Emmons then made a series of introductions, including school board secretary Fred Hums, Principal Russell Myers and Frank Steele, as well as Charles Cole and M.J. McErlain, the engineers involved in the project.

After the pregame festivities had concluded, it was time for the main event, and both teams took the field. In the first half, neither side generated much offense. The Maroons had only 10 yards on the ground and 35 in the air, but they made the most of their best scoring chance. Near the end of the second quarter, Heftie passed to Andy Van de Putte, good for a 19-yard gain that put the ball on the Riley 14. With the period's last seconds ticking away and no time for a pass or run, Joe Gall dropped back to the 25-yard line and kicked a field goal straight through the uprights.

At halftime, both schools' bands performed. The Mishawaka band, directed by Max Kraning, played "Over the Rainbow," the popular song from the year's hit movie *The Wizard of Oz*. The stadium lights were turned off to create a dark background, and the band formed into a rainbow with colors provided by small lights on the musicians' hats. As the band members marched back and forth, the rainbow appeared to move, an effect that brought enthusiastic applause. When the lights were again turned on, saxophonist Helen Guin sang a chorus of the song. The musicians then performed "Roll Out the Barrel," the school fight song, while in the shape of a revolving *M*; "The Notre Dame Victory March"; and several other songs.

After the players returned to the gridiron for the second half, Riley's only scoring threat came midway through the fourth quarter after Heftie's pass was intercepted and returned to the Mishawaka 31. The Wildcats made small gains on the next two plays, but an interception by Gall killed the drive. In his final game as a Caveman, Gall was outstanding. In addition to the field goal and interception, he "was a fifth man in the Wildcats' backfield all night, and Coach Forrest M. Wood's lads just couldn't seem to get anything started but what Gall was horning in," wrote Wendell Jollieff. Mishawaka emerged victorious, 3–0.

The *Enterprise* gave rave reviews for the evening's entertainment, its headline declaring, "Dedication Event Is Huge Success." The paper described the pregame ceremony and halftime performance as "one of the most thrilling programs in the history of Mishawaka High School athletics" and added that the narrow win "was, of course, the crowning touch to a successful program."

Mishawaka's 4-5-1 record was disappointing, but the Cavemen's spirited play, tough defense and game-winning scores had given their fans much to be proud of. The heroics of Harry Heftie, Larry Deal, Joe Gall and their teammates provided thrilling memories, but the real star of the 1939 season was the Maroons' beautiful stadium, which offered the promise of greater achievements to come.

Although it has long been popular to borrow the language of warfare to describe football games, the reality is that the boys who competed at Mishawaka's School Field in the autumn of 1939 were still just playing a game. The real winds of war were nonetheless swirling about, and many of these young men would soon be wearing steel helmets instead of leather and trading in their cleats and shoulder pads for guns and bayonets.

Three of the 1939 Maroons made the ultimate sacrifice during World War II: LaVern Trittipo, Jack Deal and Charles La Vine.

Private First Class LaVern Trittipo, class of 1942, served in the 2nd Marine Division, fought on Tarawa and was killed in action in the South Pacific on June 15, 1944, three weeks short of his twentieth birthday. Private First Class Trittipo is buried at the National Memorial Cemetery of the Pacific in Honolulu, Hawaii.

Private First Class LaVern Trittipo is buried in Hawaii. A memorial marker honors him at Chapel Hill Memorial Gardens, Osceola. *Author's collection.*

Sergeant Jack Deal, class of 1941, was an armorer-gunner on a B-24 Liberator based in Italy with the 455th Bombardment Group, 15th Air Force. Deal was killed on October 13, 1944, when his bomber took a direct hit from flak over the Blechhammer oil refineries in German-occupied southwestern Poland. The aircraft broke in two, and between three and five parachutes were reported coming from the plane. Jack was usually a tailgunner, but on this mission he manned the ball-turret, which allowed no emergency egress. Two crewmen from the plane were captured and interned at a German prisoner-of-war camp. According to an Individual Casualty Questionnaire later filled out by the surviving tailgunner, "Some member of another crew told my nose gunner while in prison camp that he seen the ball turrett [*sic*] go sailing down by itself." Deal had been listed as missing in action until the War Department confirmed his death in February 1945. His remains were recovered from a common grave in Upper Silesia and positively identified in January 1956. Sergeant Deal was reinterred at Chapel Hill Memorial Gardens, Osceola.

Aviation Machinist Mate Second Class Charles La Vine, class of 1941, died of wounds in the Pacific on March 14, 1945. He had worked at the Kingsbury Ordnance Plant before joining the U.S. Navy in 1942. Surviving

Jack Deal in his U.S. Army Air Force uniform. *Pastor Greg Lawson.*

La Vine were his wife and their nine-month-old son, Michael. Aviation Mate La Vine is buried at Etna Green East Cemetery, northwest of Warsaw.

At least thirty-one of Trittipo, Deal and La Vine's teammates also served in the United States military, many experiencing combat.

Chick Maggioli, a member of Notre Dame's 1943 national championship team, had to leave school in late October 1944 when he was called to active duty with the Marine Corps. Private First Class Maggioli received a Purple Heart after an explosion blew him off a bridge in Okinawa. He survived the war, completed his college career at the University of Illinois and played three seasons in the National Football League.

A list of other veterans from the 1939 football team makes for an impressive record of wartime service. Staff Sergeant Joe Gall was a member of the 99th Infantry Division and fought in the Battle of the Bulge, Staff Sergeant Wayne Linson served in the 78th Infantry Division and was awarded a Purple Heart after being wounded in Germany and Corporal Larry Deal was a medic serving with General George Patton's 3rd Army in Belgium at the time of his older brother Jack's death. Sergeant Bob Wachs was in the 11th Airborne Division, which participated in liberating the Philippines in late 1944 and early 1945, and Corporal Kenneth Koontz fought in the South

Pacific. Staff Sergeant Charles Rupchock was stationed with the engineering corps at Santa Fe, New Mexico, and worked on the Manhattan Project at Los Alamos. Sergeant Arnold Thompson served as an Army Air Force gunnery instructor in Las Vegas, Nevada. Staff Sergeant Richard Good and Sergeant Julius De Vreese were also in the Army Air Force. Among the other U.S. Army veterans were Technician Third Grade Andy Van de Putte, who served in the 5th Ordnance Medium Maintenance Company; Staff Sergeant Fred Meuninck; Corporal Bill Stockberger; Corporal Tom Baiz; Corporal George Pozwilka; and Private First Class Charles Kopsea. Army enlistment records also include Dale Moore, William Carnes, Lloyd Katterheinrich and Camiel De Volder. Lieutenant Bob Herron was a navy fighter pilot, Ensign George Muinch flew a dive bomber in the navy and Seaman Albert Hums was stationed on USS *Kenmore* in the Pacific and received a Purple Heart. Fireman First Class Harry Heftie, Seaman Second Class William Potts, Seaman Second Class Larry Savage and Seaman Second Class Troy Williams also served in the navy. Sergeant Frank Severa was in the Marine Corps and fought on Guadalcanal. Second Lieutenant John Richardson and Private First Class Herbert Hoffman were also in the Marines. The Mishawaka-Penn-Harris Public Library's Heritage Center has a document that lists 4,500 Mishawakans who served in the armed forces during World War II. Among them is also Clarence Houghton.

Several luminaries in the history of Mishawaka athletics were associated with the 1939 football team. Five men were later inducted into the Mishawaka High School Athletic Hall of Fame. Russell Arndt, Walter Thurston, Frank Steele and Chick Maggioli were part of the inaugural class in 1986, and Joe Gall joined them in 1995. Raymond Struck, who had also coached the Maroons' basketball team to a sectional title in 1939 and went on to be a coach and longtime athletic director at Hanover College, was inducted into the Indiana Football Hall of Fame in 1974 and the Indiana Basketball Hall of Fame in 1977.

The years passed and life moved on for everyone who played in or watched the games at School Field during the 1939 season. Even the sturdy stadium was not immune to the vicissitudes of time. After William Tupper retired from the school board in July 1941, School City honored him and his twenty-two years of service by changing Mishawaka High School Stadium to Tupper Field. A renovation project in 1980 added an all-weather track, new light poles behind the bleachers and a replacement for the original press box. These improvements prompted School City to rename the facility Frank M. Steele Stadium in September 1980. Other changes occurred in the following years, such as installing modern goalposts, sealing the concrete bleachers, putting in aluminum seats, painting the stands white and later maroon and grey, erecting new fencing and brick columns and constructing Alumni Plaza at the stadium's southwest entrance. Most recently, substantial upgrades occurred in 2017–18: new light poles, a state-of-the-art track surface, a free-standing video scoreboard and an expanded Alumni Plaza.

Since they were completed and dedicated in the fall of 1939, the WPA-built bleachers at Mishawaka High's football field have witnessed much history. In addition to the Cavemen's games, they were used for the great Marian High teams of the 1960s and '70s before Otolski Field was constructed. The stands have also seen track meets, pep rallies, commencements, marching band practices and physical education classes. Nearly every person who has lived in Mishawaka for any substantial time—and thousands of visitors to the city—has been a participant or spectator at an event held in this stadium.

What eventually became Steele Stadium had its genesis in the vision of Superintendent P.C. Emmons and the pen of President Franklin Roosevelt. Emmons knew that concrete bleachers built by the WPA would facilitate the success of Cavemen football teams, which would engender community support for Mishawaka High. Roosevelt, though, had little thought of football games or a particular school when he signed the authorizations for School Field's east and west bleachers. He was more concerned about providing jobs and hope to the unemployed, stimulating the economy and building recreational infrastructure in an industrial city recovering from the Great Depression. When President Roosevelt approved WPA funds for School Field, he was investing in peace and prosperity. What he could not know at the time, though, was that he was also funding the nation's preparation for war by encouraging the physical fitness and team-building of young men who would soon face the rigors of military service.

Local and federal governments spent roughly $130,000 (in 1938–39 dollars) to construct the stadium's bleachers. Considering the cost, use and longevity of these stands, few structures in the city's history can compare with such a return on taxpayer investment. If properly maintained, this Mishawaka landmark should endure for at least another eighty years, evoking thoughts of gridiron battles past and a world at war. It will also be the setting for future generations to write their own chapters of the stadium's still-unfolding history.

CHAPTER 7

MISHAWAKA HIGH SCHOOL FOOTBALL'S TWENTY GREATEST HOME WINS, 1939–2018

I n celebration of the eightieth anniversary of the WPA bleachers at Steele Stadium, Mishawaka faithful should remember the Cavemen's twenty greatest home football wins since 1939.

October 6, 1939
Mishawaka 12, Goshen 0
In the first two home games between the WPA bleachers, Mishawaka had a 0–0 tie and a 6–0 loss to its credit, and the next two weeks on the road resulted in two more defeats. For the Maroon faithful wondering when they would be able to cheer for the first Mishawaka points in the new stadium, their wait ended in the second quarter. Harry Heftie's 53-yard run, dodging and straight-arming Redskin defenders, ended with a goal line tackle and a skid into the end zone. The Cavemen scored again late in the third quarter after Heftie's interception on the Goshen 37-yard line. Five plays later, Larry Deal ran 7 yards for a touchdown, and Mishawaka had its first home win of the season.

October 20, 1950
Mishawaka 13, Elkhart 6
Possibly an all-time record crowd of ten thousand people watched Mishawaka and Elkhart play scoreless ball through three quarters. In the first half, the Maroons had failed to make a single first down, and the Blue Blazers'

Left: Bob Sriver carries around Elkhart's left end. *Mishawaka Historical Museum.*

Right: Coach Gene Dykstra inspires his team at halftime of the Peoria game. *Mishawaka Historical Museum.*

most promising drives were stopped on a fumble and interception. After a scoreless third quarter, the game-winning points for the Maroons came as Veryl Stamm pounded into the end zone from 1 yard out. Mishawaka added to its lead on a 13-yard touchdown run by Bob Sriver, but Elkhart could only muster a late touchdown. The Cavemen went on to finish 9–1, won the Northern Indiana High School Conference championship playoff and claimed the mythical state championship.

October 5, 1951
Mishawaka 14, Peoria (Illinois) Manual 0
In front of eight thousand fans, Mishawaka ended Manual's twenty-eight-game winning streak. After both teams were shut out in the first half, a Ram fumble on their own 37 led to the decisive score, an 18-yard pass from Bob Sriver to Chuck Mikulyuk. The Maroons built on their lead in the fourth quarter after Mikulyuk and Bill Stricker recovered another Manual fumble on the Rams' 20. Five plays later, Jack Benjamin smashed across the goal line on a 1-yard run.

Jim Kocsis (*top*) and Ray Bolin (*bottom*) bring down a Central runner. *Mishawaka Historical Museum.*

November 6, 1953
Mishawaka 14, South Bend Central 6
Enduring temperatures in the low twenties, neither team had been able to put any points on the board in the first half. Mishawaka broke the frozen tie midway through the third quarter as it drove down field, and Danny Ransberger rushed into the end zone from 7 yards out. After Central scored to end the stanza, the Cavemen marched 65 yards on eight running plays, and Ray Bolin capped off the drive by maneuvering over the goal line. The Bears had no answer, and Mishawaka went on to claim its thirteenth victory over Central—against twenty-four losses and four ties—and the first in a game played at Tupper Field.

October 21, 1960
Mishawaka 20, South Bend Central 6
Central fumbled on its own 25 early in the second quarter, and Mishawaka promptly scored after a pass by John Coppens and 15-yard and 1-yard runs by Tom Fern. Another Bruin fumble thirty seconds before halftime led to the Maroons' second touchdown. Rich Witkowski, substituting for Coppens, fired a pass from the 24-yard line to Dick Bortone, who caught it on the 8, evaded a defender and scampered into the end zone. In the fourth quarter, a blocked Central punt soon resulted in Witkowski's second touchdown throw, a 13-yard strike to Dick Nelson. Celebrating the first win over their archrival in four years, Mishawaka students tore down both goalposts, a first for Tupper Field.

September 8, 1972
Mishawaka 60, Penn 6
The Kingsmen got on the board early with an 85-yard touchdown run, but Mishawaka soon responded, finding the goal line on a 29-yard pitchout play from John Marzotto to John Van Bruaene. The Cavemen scored at will from then on, leading 28–6 at the half and adding five touchdowns in the second half. Mishawaka's twenty-two first downs and 377 yards rushing were aided by an interception and six Penn fumbles. The lopsided win was the high

point of Mishawaka's early dominance over Penn and one of the largest margins of victory in Cavemen history. Later generations of fans have found this score difficult to believe.

September 7, 1973
Mishawaka 22, Marian 15
Marian took the early lead and was threatening again in the second quarter when Mishawaka stopped them on the 1-yard line. The Cavemen then went 99 yards, twice recovering Knight fumbles on punts, to score on Mike Breske's 10-yard pass to Rob Morin on a tackle-eligible play. Marian retook the lead early in the fourth quarter, but Mishawaka answered with a long drive that ended with Breske's 1-yard dive and then a 2-point conversion by Breske to Lou Mihajlovich. Marian tied the game at 15 with 1:25 remaining, but the Cavemen moved quickly down the field and scored on Breske's 4-yard pass to Scot Shaw. Marian went on to win the Class A state championship.

November 9, 1974
Mishawaka 28, Portage 21
After a scoreless first quarter, Larry Roberts's 1-yard run completed the first of three consecutive Cavemen scoring drives. Chuck Alexander's 2-yard touchdown run and Dale Moore's 11-yard scoring throw to Mike DeGeeter gave Mishawaka a 21–6 lead at the half. When the Indians fumbled on their own 11 midway through the third quarter, Kim Davis recovered and

Mishawaka players carry the playoff trophy and chant, "We're number 1!" after defeating Portage. *Mishawaka Historical Museum.*

advanced the ball to the 2, and Alexander shot into the end zone on the next play. Portage answered with two touchdowns, but it was not enough. The 10–1 Cavemen's playoff win advanced them to the Class AAA state championship game.

August 26, 1977
Mishawaka 28, South Bend St. Joseph's 27
After St. Joseph's scored first near the end of the opening quarter, Mishawaka tied the game midway through the second quarter on a 1-yard dive by John Roggeman. Jim Aldrich's 2-yard touchdown run gave the Cavemen the lead, but the Indians made it 14–14 just before halftime. St. Joseph's extended their lead to 27–14, and Roggeman's 2-yard plunge into the end zone helped bring the Cavemen to within 6 just before the third quarter expired. With 2:15 left in the game, Aldrich's 6-yard run tied the game, and Dennis Teegarden, the son of St. Joseph's coach Phil Teegarden, kicked the game-winning extra point.

October 28, 1977
Mishawaka 21, South Bend Washington 13
Nine thousand fans watched two undefeated teams battle in the regular season finale. Mishawaka struck first with a 19-yard pass from Mike Henke to Tim Settles. Washington was stopped on downs near the Cavemen goal line, and Mishawaka then moved steadily down the field. John Roggeman's 24-yard run gave the hosts a 14–0 lead, but the Panthers rallied with two touchdowns. A failed 2-point attempt maintained the Cavemen's slim lead, which they added to on a 2-yard touchdown run by Jim Aldrich. Mishawaka finished the regular season 10–0 and won the Northern Indiana Conference championship. The following week, the Cavemen lost a heartbreaking playoff rematch with the Panthers.

September 26, 1980
Mishawaka 35, Penn 32
One of the all-time best Mishawaka teams got everything it could handle from Penn, which took an early lead after a nine-minute opening drive. In the second quarter, Mishawaka scored three times on John Coppens's 17-yard pass to Ted Carlson, a 69-yard throw to Dan Frederick and a 1-yard run by Rob Bloomer. A 72-yard touchdown pass from Coppens to Brett Candler in the third quarter and Coppens's 1-yard run in the fourth built the Cavemen lead to 35–24, but Penn scored again to close within

Mishawaka celebrates as the final second ticks off in the 35–32 win over Penn. *Mishawaka Historical Museum.*

3. The Kingsmen were driving with under a minute to play when Randy Usenick's interception sealed the win. This was Mishawaka's last win over Penn until 2009.

October 10, 1980
Mishawaka 7, Elkhart Central 0
Undefeated and number 1–ranked Mishawaka faced a strong challenge from unbeaten Elkhart Central. Three quarters of outstanding defense had prevented either team from scoring. In the fourth quarter, though, John Coppens used a mix of throws to Rob Bloomer and runs by Jay Plummer to advance from the Cavemen 49 to the Blue Blazer 1-yard line. Coppens then broke through the right side and into the end zone for the go-ahead score. Central drove to the Mishawaka 3-yard line but gave up the ball on downs with thirty-two seconds to play. The Cavemen later completed a 10-0 regular season, won the conference title and made the AAA playoffs.

October 22, 1982
Mishawaka 13, Elkhart Central 12
Mishawaka's defense rose to the occasion to upset the favored Blue Blazers. Elkhart had stifled the Cavemen offense and led 12–0 in the third quarter

when Dan Morrow intercepted a Blue Blazer lateral and raced 65 yards for a touchdown. Penalties had pinned Central deep in Mishawaka territory when Tod Meersman picked off a pass and returned it to the Blazer 15 with 2:06 remaining in the game. Three plays later, the ball was on the 3 when Tom Gaby faked a handoff and ran into the end zone for the winning touchdown. This win and a victory over Clay the next week gave Mishawaka, 9-1, a share of the conference championship and another berth in the AAA playoffs.

November 2, 1990
Mishawaka 16, Valparaiso 14
After trailing 7–0 at halftime, Mishawaka tied the game on a 16-yard run by Jerry Dominiack. Valparaiso retook the lead in the fourth quarter, but the Cavemen cut the deficit to 2 points after Kevin Cousins's 5-yard run and a failed 2-point conversion with fifty-five seconds remaining. For the first time all season, the Cavemen tried an onside kick, and they recovered the ball on the Vikings' 46. A 26-yard completion from Cory Betzer to Steve Shedd set up Craig Lanning's game-winning 36-yard field goal as time expired. With this victory, Mishawaka, 9-2, had its second 5A sectional title in three years.

November 15, 1991
Mishawaka 14, Crown Point 7
Matt Mammolenti's 4-yard touchdown run thirty seconds before halftime lifted Mishawaka to a 7–0 lead. After Crown Point tied the game late in the third quarter, the Cavemen replied with a drive capped off by Mammolenti's 1-yard dive. Mishawaka got the ball back with 7:07 left in the game, and Cory Betzer used an effective passing attack to lead the Cavemen down field, killing the clock and the Bulldogs' hopes for a comeback. Mishawaka, 9-3, had defeated Portage, Valparaiso and Crown Point in consecutive weeks to claim its first regional title and earn a trip to the 5A semi-state game.

October 2, 2009
Mishawaka 26, Penn 10
A first-quarter fumble by number 1–ranked Penn led to the Cavemen's initial score, an 18-yard pass from Cortez Lee to Justin Frazier. Penn soon reclaimed the lead, 7–6, but Mishawaka replied with a 68-yard drive, climaxed by Lee's 4-yard scamper and Gary Brooks's run for a 2-point conversion. Penn added a field goal before halftime but did not score again. The Cavemen dominated the third quarter with a 9:21 drive that ended in Lee's 13-yard touchdown run. The final blow came with 4:15 left in the game as Lee bolted for a 41-

yard score. The victory snapped a thirty-five-game losing streak to Penn. Many alumni not in attendance that historic night can still describe vividly the moment they learned that Mishawaka had finally beaten Penn.

November 6, 2009
Mishawaka 24, Penn 21
Mishawaka and Penn had a rematch later that season for the 5A sectional championship, and the Cavemen had a chance to prove that the earlier upset was no fluke. Mishawaka surged to a 17–0 lead on a 29-yard Matt Reisdorf field goal, Tyler Reinoehl's 11-yard scoring run and Cortez Lee's 22-yard touchdown pass to P.J. Warmouth. The Kingsmen answered with a touchdown before halftime and two more in the third quarter. With just under five minutes to go in the game, Mishawaka got the ball back and found the end zone on a 50-yard run by Reinoehl. When Penn's field goal attempt failed with forty-two seconds remaining, Mishawaka, 11-1, began celebrating its first sectional title since 1991.

November 5, 2010
Mishawaka 14, Penn 7
After having defeated its nemesis for the third straight time earlier in the season at Freed Field, undefeated Mishawaka again faced Penn for the sectional championship. Both teams were scoreless in the first half, and the Kingsmen took the lead in the third quarter. The Cavemen then moved 87 yards down the field and tied the game with 5.6 seconds remaining in regulation on Kevin Day's 6-yard touchdown run. In the dramatic overtime, Sam Schrader ran 2 yards for the go-ahead touchdown, and Ben Versyp tackled the Penn quarterback at the 10-yard line on the final play to secure Mishawaka's second consecutive 5A sectional title.

November 9, 2012
Mishawaka 39, Hammond Morton 7
Playing for the 4A regional championship, Mishawaka scored first on Sam Schrader's 34-yard pass to Matt Carver. Daniel Blackford's 27-yard field goal and Schrader's 2-yard touchdown run built an 18–7 lead by halftime. The Cavemen ruled the Governors in the second half as touchdowns from Tyler McDaniel's 14-yard run, Schrader's 23-yard pass to Carver and Evan Fras's 1-yard run turned the game into a blowout. Mishawaka, 10-3, next traveled to Concord for the semi-state, won a thriller and advanced to the state championship game for the first time since 1974.

November 9, 2018
Mishawaka 28, Lowell 14
With snow covering the field and snowflakes swirling under the lights, Steele Stadium looked like a snow globe as Mishawaka had to contain the offense of two-time defending regional champion Lowell. The Cavemen struck first on Chris Harness's 15-yard touchdown run and took a 7–0 lead into halftime. After a Red Devils touchdown, Mishawaka answered with another drive, finished off by Harness's 1-yard run. With the score tied at 14 and eight minutes remaining, Sam Shively threw to Bradley Taylor, who raced 34 yards into the end zone. Harness put the game out of reach on a 77-yard run with under two minutes to go. The Cavemen, 12-1, had captured their first 4A regional title since 2012.

CHAPTER 8

FROM MISHAWAKA TO TOKYO

Ball-Band and the Doolittle Raid

Mishawaka's role in helping the United States achieve victory in World War II included the wartime service of 4,500 of its citizens, the ultimate sacrifice of 105 military personnel and the labor of thousands of defense workers in the city's factories. An important war event to which Mishawaka industry contributed was the Doolittle Raiders' April 18, 1942 attack on Tokyo, the first air strike by the United States against the Japanese home islands.

The raid had its origins in a December 21, 1941 meeting in which President Franklin Roosevelt ordered the Joint Chiefs of Staff to bomb Japan as retaliation for the December 7 attack on Pearl Harbor. A raid on its cities would damage Japan's war-making capability and undermine the Japanese people's faith in their government.

Roosevelt had told the military to hit Japan, but the operational specifics of how to do this were still to be determined. Three weeks later, U.S. Navy captain Francis Low informed Admiral Ernest King, commander of the U.S. Fleet, that he believed twin-engine U.S. Army bombers could be launched off the deck of an aircraft carrier to hit targets in Japan. Low had observed planes at Norfolk, Virginia, practicing takeoffs from a runway painted to the dimensions of a carrier deck.

The bombers selected to undertake the mission would need to launch from a carrier, hit targets in Japan and then fly on to airfields in China or the Soviet Union. General Henry "Hap" Arnold, chief of the Army Air Corps, had his staff—including former racing pilot, aviation pioneer and then lieutenant colonel Jimmy Doolittle—evaluate bombers for possible use in such a mission. Selection criteria included being able to take off in an area five hundred feet long and less than seventy-five feet wide, carry two tons of bombs and fly two thousand miles with a complete crew. While the army's B-23 and B-25 bombers could both carry the desired bomb load and, if modified, have the range to do the mission, the B-25's wingspan of sixty-seven feet was short enough that it would not hit a carrier's superstructure and would leave room to fit at least sixteen planes on the deck. The B-25 had a crew of just five officers and enlisted men.

Arnold tasked Doolittle with modifying the bombers and training the crews to carry out an attack on Japan sometime between mid-April and mid-May, the period when weather would be most favorable over Tokyo. Meanwhile, USS *Hornet*, completing its shakedown cruise in the Caribbean, would transit the Panama Canal to Alameda Naval Air Station near San Francisco, where it would await the airmen and their B-25s.

Doolittle began planning the formidable logistics of the top-secret operation, which he called "Special Aviation Project No. 1." He expected the B-25s would take off from *Hornet* 500 miles east of Tokyo, keeping the navy vessels out of range of Japanese land-based aircraft, and fly another 1,200 miles to China. Doolittle calculated that any bomber's longest nonstop flight would be 2,000 miles, but he wanted a cruising range of 2,400 miles, to be safe. Each aircraft would carry four five-hundred-pound bombs: three demolition bombs and one incendiary cluster consisting of 128 bomblets that would be spread over an area of two hundred by six hundred square feet and set fire to Japanese buildings that were made mostly of wood and paper.

Doolittle's "most critical modification," according James Scott in his book *Target Tokyo*, would be to almost double the B-25's normal range of 1,300 miles by adding fuel tanks squeezed inside the aircraft's cabin. The B-25 had two wing tanks that held 646 gallons, but Doolittle needed the aircraft to carry almost 500 more gallons than it was designed for. Adding to the fuel conundrum was that each extra gallon of fuel increased the plane's weight by six pounds and lengthened the distance needed for a safe takeoff. A fully loaded B-25 weighed thirty-one thousand pounds and would consume 78 gallons of fuel per hour.

Mishawaka Rubber & Woolen Company, a subsidiary of United States Rubber Company, would play a vital part in solving the B-25's fuel capacity problem and ensuring the Doolittle Raid's success. The company, better known as Ball-Band, had already demonstrated proficiency in developing fuel cells for military aircraft before receiving the order for the Doolittle B-25s. For more than a year, the Mishawaka plant had been making self-sealing fuel cells for Glenn L. Martin Company's B-26 Marauder. Martin had patented this type of fuel cell, known as a Mareng ("Mar" for Martin and "eng" for engineering) in 1937, and U.S. Rubber had acquired the exclusive rights to manufacture these cells in July 1940.

In January 1942, the Army Air Corps' power plant laboratory at Wright Field in Ohio needed to expand the fuel capacity of the B-17 Flying Fortress. After a meeting between George Blair, manager of the Mishawaka plant's development laboratories, and Captain George Smith from Wright Field, U.S. Rubber committed to build three fuel cells to go in an outer wing cavity that had never previously been used for fuel storage. Within three days, the fuel cells and their fittings were at Wright Field for a test installment. Pleased with the product, the army ordered ten self-sealing cells for each wing of a B-17, an order that Ball-Band filled within ten days. All forms, fittings and metal parts for the fuel cells had to be quickly made in the Ball-Band shops. The cells increased the B-17's fuel capacity by 1,100 gallons, giving planes enough range to bomb Japanese-held islands from bases in Australia.

Soon after the Mishawaka factory had completed this test order in January 1942, Wright Field contacted Martin Company to make fuel cells to expand the fuel capacity of twenty-six B-25s that would be used in a secret mission. The Army Air Corps asked for a flexible fuel cell that could fit in a specific space within a B-25. Colonel Frank Cook told Martin engineers, "We want as much gasoline as you can get into the crawlway of the B-25."

On February 1, 1942, officers from the Army Air Corps production engineering branch met with Martin engineers and Ball-Band's Virgil Van Dinter and Fred Sawyer at Wright Field to discuss developing Mareng fuel cells for the B-25s, similar to what had been done with the B-17s. When George Blair was then asked if the Mishawaka plant could complete the special order, he responded, "There's a war on! We'll do it."

According to an article in the Pacific Aviation Museum's magazine *NOTAM*, Doolittle himself "hand carried" orders for the fuel cells to Mishawaka with a firm delivery date of March 15—there could be no extensions.

Using Martin Company plans, Ball-Band was tasked with manufacturing two fuel cells that would be placed within the existing B-25 airframe. The tight cabin configuration of the B-25 did not allow for just one additional fuel tank, so engineers at Wright Field and Martin had to create different sizes of tanks that could fit into available spaces inside the aircraft. At first, a 265-gallon steel tank was developed by McQuay Company but it leaked

Ball-Band workers are making fuel cells similar to those that enabled the Doolittle Raiders to attack Tokyo and fly on to China. *Mishawaka-Penn-Harris Public Library.*

badly, and Doolittle later rejected the tank in favor of a 225-gallon self-sealing, bulletproof fuel cell made by Ball-Band. The tank would fit in the top of the bomb bay yet allow enough space for the four bombs. Martin engineers quickly designed a second 160-gallon flexible synthetic rubber bladder that, when filled with fuel, would completely occupy the crawlway that connected the cabin and the aft fuselage, the structure of which would support the weight of the fuel load so that no stress was on the bag itself. After the fuel was used, crew members could flatten the empty tank, allowing the engineer-gunner to move forward. This cell was also made by Ball-Band.

Much more challenging to construct was the fuel tank for the bomb bay. In his *History of the Fuel Cell Division, United States Rubber Company, 1940–1945,* George Newitt noted that the company "had never before built plastic housings" and had to quickly develop new methods for making them. Likewise, the self-sealing cells, their metal compression fittings and building forms all had to be fabricated at the Ball-Band plant. The fuel cell, carpenter and machine shops adopted a twenty-four-hour, seven-day schedule to complete the order within the absolute timetable that Doolittle demanded. The self-sealing cells had a Thiokol liner, spread latex sealant and gum rubber retainer. When the Thiokol supply began to run low, some of the tanks had to be made with Saflex plastic lining. Because Saflex was available only in eight-inch-wide sheets, they had to be spliced to create the liners. The plastic support housings for the fuel cells were made from U.S. Rubber's S.S. Board, a thermoplastic material that could be shaped as needed and then joined with rivets.

According to historian Bernard Rice, who worked at Ball-Band during World War II, the fuel cells were made on the fourth floor of a building that stood along the west side of Main Street, just south of the Main Street Bridge. The building also included a fuel cell lab. Four hundred young men, mostly high school students or recent graduates, worked in the fuel cell division, which came to be called "Boys Town."

During the intense weeks when the Doolittle order was being completed, the fuel cell division ran continuously, "with engineers, draftsmen, supervisors, and older men working as long as 36 hours at a stretch," wrote Rice. "They designed wooden molds, like jigsaw puzzles, to be taken apart and removed from inside the fuel cell after the rubber had been cured in a vulcanizer."

As the fuel cells were developed, Lieutenant Colonel Doolittle visited the Mishawaka plant multiple times. Despite his presence and the special nature and urgency of the project, none of the Ball-Band workers knew the details of the secret mission in which they were so vitally involved.

When ready for test-fitting, some finished cells were flown to Wold-Chamberlain Field in Minneapolis. After a few final changes, Doolittle arrived in Minneapolis to oversee the installation of the test tanks. In twenty-five-below weather early the next morning, he watched as the tank was filled with one-hundred-octane fuel. When the cell initially seemed to hold half a gallon below its intended capacity, Doolittle mounted a ladder and shook the B-25's tail up and down. The action sloshed the fuel enough that the tank could take one more gallon, enough to put it half a gallon over the specifications. To complete the test, Doolittle then climbed into the cockpit to sniff for gas fumes. Mareng cell seams had cemented strips to make them liquid-tight, and these had been reinforced when the tanks were fitted. Satisfied by the lack of fuel aroma, Doolittle smiled and noted that he wanted to make sure his fliers could smoke during their long flight.

En route to the next phase of mission preparation and crew training at Eglin Field in Florida, the B-25s flew from Minneapolis to Bendix Field in South Bend to acquire the remaining Ball-Band fuel tanks.

The Ball-Band fuel cell housings made in Mishawaka were used in the B-25s that bombed Tokyo during the Doolittle Raid. *Mishawaka-Penn-Harris Public Library.*

The full order of fifty-two fuel tanks and twenty-six plastic housings was complete and delivered by the date Doolittle had set when he had visited the Mishawaka facility. Doolittle also had made the arrangements for the tanks to be delivered to the B-25 pilots at Bendix Field. Ball-Band personnel went to Florida to help the army install the fuel cells.

As the Doolittle Raiders were practicing short-distance takeoffs and over-ocean navigation in their aircraft at Eglin Field, they discovered that the crawlway bladder cell and bomb bay tanks were not providing enough fuel capacity. According to Newitt, this was partly due to the bomb bay housings

Fuel cells made at Ball-Band were installed when the B-25s were at Eglin Field, Florida, in March 1942. *U.S. Army.*

being too small for the cells, causing them to buckle and fold inside the housing and limit the amount of fuel they could hold.

Lieutenant Colonel Doolittle asked Fred Sawyer at Ball-Band to solve the problem of the fuel cells' capacity. Sawyer's team decided to replace the small housings of the bomb bay tank, which would address the buckling and allow more fuel to go in the tank. A third sixty-gallon tank, also made in Mishawaka, would be stowed where the bomber's lower gun turret normally was. The belly gun had been removed to save weight and because the low-altitude nature of the mission would render it useless. With just nine days to complete these final modifications, workers in Mishawaka built two-foot cubes made of S.S. Board, each with a self-sealing cell inside. The tanks were readily manufactured from existing materials, forms and fittings.

Each bomber would also have ten 5-gallon fuel cans that were kept in the radio operator's rear compartment and would be jettisoned after they had been used. According to Carroll Glines's *The Doolittle Raid*, the rear gunner would refill the 60-gallon tank with these cans. After all these alterations had been made, Doolittle's bombers could each carry a total of 1,141 gallons of fuel.

"Again the Fuel Cell Department was turned upside down to complete twenty-four self-sealing cells and plastic housings in the time allotted," wrote Newitt. Doolittle sent special planes to Bendix Field to pick up the new cells and housings, which were then transported to McLellan Field in Sacramento, California, where the B-25s had been flown from Florida.

Doolittle's own report on the Tokyo Raid, dated June 5, 1942, explains, "Considerable difficulty was experienced with this [225-gallon] rubber bullet-proof tank due to leaks in the connections and due to the fact that after having made one fairly satisfactory tank, the outer case was reduced in size in order to facilitate installation without reducing the size of the inner rubber container, and consequently wrinkles developed reducing the capacity and increasing the tendency for failure and leakage." Doolittle went on to explain that pressurizing the tank added ten to fifteen gallons of capacity.

Fred Sawyer was in Sacramento to oversee the installation of the sixty-gallon tanks, housings and other repairs on the crawlway and bomb bay tanks. Within six hours, twenty-four fuel cubes were installed, and all of the cells and housings were in the aircraft by March 25. An undated handwritten letter from Sawyer to George Blair, on stationery from a Sacramento hotel, reads, "Col. Doolittle is here and I believe will lead the ships on planned mission. I will stay until ships leave here or job is finished."

Ball-Band's Virgil Van Dinter, too, helped ensure the timely and successful completion of the order for Doolittle's mission. Van Dinter flew a total of nine thousand miles while meeting with personnel from the Army Air Corps, North American Aviation and Martin Aircraft and assisting with the fuel cells' installation.

Another Mishawakan and fuel cell division employee, Bob LeMon, was also at McClellan Field, where he spent six days helping Army Air Corps mechanics install hoses to the fuel cells on the B-25s that would attack Japan. On the seventh day, according to *NOTAM*, LeMon went to the airfield to continue his work, only to find the B-25s had all disappeared for an unknown destination.

At this point, Mishawaka's direct involvement in mission preparation came to an end. LeMon's missing bombers had secretly flown to Alameda NAS, where they were hoisted by crane onto the *Hornet's* deck on March 31 and April 1. The B-25s were lashed down and crowded onto the rear half of the ship's 809-foot wooden flight deck. As it sailed under the Golden

The sixteen B-25s used in the Doolittle Raid were lashed down and crowded on the rear half of the *Hornet*'s 809-foot wooden flight deck. Escort vessels can be seen in the distance. *U.S. Army.*

Gate Bridge on April 2, *Hornet* was initially accompanied by two cruisers, four destroyers and an oiler, a task force that would later be augmented by the carrier *Enterprise*, two more cruisers, four additional destroyers and another oiler. These two groups of ships would meet up northwest of Hawaii to form Task Force 16. When Admiral William "Bull" Halsey on board *Enterprise* announced, "This force is bound for Tokyo," shouts resounded throughout the ship.

The plan of attack called for the oilers to hold back while the carriers, cruisers and destroyers would steam to within 450 miles of Tokyo and launch the bombers. If the task force was sighted by Japanese ships or planes, the timetable for launch would have to be moved up in the interest of safeguarding the carriers and their escorts. Doolittle believed that his crews could still achieve their objectives if they had to launch from 550 miles, and he set 650 miles as the maximum limit. Beyond that, his Raiders would lack the fuel to reach airfields in southeastern China.

At 7:38 a.m. on April 18, lookouts on *Hornet* spotted a Japanese patrol vessel, which was able to radio Tokyo an alert about the presence of enemy aircraft carriers before an American cruiser sank the boat. Knowing that his task force had been discovered, Admiral Halsey signaled *Hornet* with the order, "Launch planes. To Col. Doolittle and gallant command, good luck and God bless you."

Hornet was more than eight hundred miles from Tokyo, nearly twice as far as Doolittle had expected. The Raiders knew that at this distance they would likely run out of fuel somewhere over the East China Sea.

The first bomber, piloted by Lieutenant Colonel Doolittle, screamed down the deck at 8:20 a.m. to the cheers of *Hornet*'s sailors and others anxiously watching from the nearby ships. With an average of four minutes between takeoffs, the other fifteen B-25s had all taken safely to the skies by 9:19 a.m. Skimming the ocean at altitudes of about two hundred feet, the planes flew individually toward the Japanese coast rather than flying in formation. Five hours after takeoff, the first B-25s were over their targets, most of which ranged across a wide swath over the urban sprawl of Tokyo and Yokohama. Three other planes flew southwest of the capital, two hitting Nagoya and a third bombing Kobe. The B-25s were spread out to create the impression of a much larger number of aircraft, to reduce the effect of enemy ground fire and fighter attacks and to enhance the element of surprise by having no plane pass over where another had previously flown.

Targets attacked included ammunition factories and armories, aircraft factories, a truck and tank factory, steel works, oil refineries and fuel tanks, power plants, army barracks and the Yokosuka Navy Yard. Fifteen of the sixteen B-25s were able to deliver their ordnance, but a sixteenth bomber was attacked by fighter planes and had to drop its bombs in the ocean.

Although the B-25s encountered anti-aircraft fire and sporadic fighter resistance, only one American plane suffered even minor damage. After bombing their targets, the Raiders turned south and flew parallel to the coast before heading west along the 29th parallel and crossing the East China Sea.

Thrilled by the raid's apparent success, Doolittle's fliers could celebrate and congratulate themselves only briefly before confronting the harsh reality of their fuel situation. Because of the premature departure from *Hornet*, it appeared they would run out of fuel between 100 and 200 miles from the Chinese coast in shark-infested and enemy-patrolled waters. Suddenly, though, the B-25s picked up a 25-mile-per-hour tailwind that would carry them nearly 1,200 miles—all the way to the coast—and undoubtedly save the lives of most of the Raiders.

The first B-25 to take off from the carrier *Hornet* was piloted by Lieutenant Colonel James H. Doolittle. *U.S. Army.*

The mission plan had called for the B-25s to land in eastern China, but here again the early takeoff created difficulties. As the navy had been unable to radio the Chinese to alert them of the planes' approach, no landing lights or flares were illuminated to guide the airmen, and darkness, rain and fog made it impossible for the Raiders to visually locate the airstrips. Instead, most crews abandoned their ships and parachuted into the night over rugged terrain, and several others crash-landed along the coast. One bomber had experienced unusually high gas consumption, causing the crew to divert to the Russian port of Vladivostok, which was just 675 miles from Tokyo. Typical of the other Raiders who reached China, Doolittle's plane was airborne for thirteen hours and covered 2,250 miles.

Of the eighty fliers who took off from the deck of the *Hornet*, two drowned when their plane crashed along the coast, and another was killed after parachuting. Eight were captured by the Japanese, three of whom were later executed. Of the remaining five prisoners, one died from starvation, and the other four remained in captivity until the war's end. The five Raiders who landed forty miles north of Vladivostok spent a year interned in the Soviet Union until they were able to escape into Iran.

Mission records and other historical accounts offer occasional references to the performance of the extra fuel tanks made in Mishawaka. According to Carroll Glines, "leaky gas tanks" on the B-25s were among the "many minor difficulties" that kept mechanics busy during their days at sea. Captain David Jones's B-25 developed a leak in the bomb bay tank the day before launching from the *Hornet*, and ship's personnel had to patch the fuel cell and keep it empty overnight. When the sudden order was given to launch the planes, crews had to quickly fill up the tank. Unfortunately, the navy had turned off the gas lines to the flight deck, forcing the B-25 to borrow gas cans from another plane until the lines were turned back on. Jones's mission report notes, "Bomb bay gas tank sprung a leak but sufficient gas was aboard to make up the loss." Despite the fuel tank problems, his crew was able to complete the mission and safely bailed out near Chuchow. Lieutenant William Bower's engineering report on four aircraft stated, "Special bomb bay tank was unsatisfactory in one case. The inner lining ruptured with result that the tank leaked in spite of all attempts to repair it. Venting system of crawlway tank was satisfactory only under daylight conditions." Lieutenant Richard Knobloch's report on four of the B-25s also made brief reference to the fuel tanks: "Bomb-bay, turret, crawlway, and wing tanks gave satisfactory performance."

For all their training and sacrifices, what had the Doolittle Raiders accomplished in their attack? Japanese reports show that the B-25s destroyed 112 buildings and damaged another 53 structures. In terms of casualties, 87 people—mostly civilians—were killed, 151 were severely injured and at least 311 had minor injuries. Military and industrial targets had been destroyed, but the size of the attack—just sixty bombs—had little material effect on Japan's war-making capabilities. Compared to later American bombing campaigns that would obliterate and incinerate Japan's cities, the actual destruction caused by the Doolittle Raiders was small and temporary. The raid's greatest effect on the Japanese people was psychological: it shattered the aura of the home islands' invulnerability to aerial attack. As a result, the Japanese government redirected more resources—such as fighter planes and anti-aircraft guns—to the defense of its cities and away from the combat theaters where they would otherwise have been deployed. The raid also led the Japanese Imperial Army to reverse its earlier refusal to participate in an attack on the American base at Midway in the central Pacific. The Battle of Midway in June 1942 would result in a decisive Japanese defeat, including the loss of four aircraft carriers. For the remainder of the war, Japan would be on the defensive as American forces' island-hopping brought them ever closer and eventually within the range of B-29s that would rain destruction from the skies over Japan.

The most devastating consequence of the Doolittle Raid occurred not in Japan, but in eastern China, where the Japanese carried out a brutal three-month series of reprisals known as the Zhejiang-Jiangxi Campaign. The Japanese Imperial Army destroyed military bases and the airfields the Raiders had hoped to use, tortured to death anyone known to have aided the American fliers, slaughtered every person in villages through which the Raiders traveled, flattened cities with tens of thousands of inhabitants and used biological warfare against civilians. An estimated 250,000 Chinese lives were lost as part of the Japanese retaliation for the Doolittle Raid.

The United States government was slow to acknowledge the raid or to discuss any details. Hoping to protect the *Hornet*'s safety and to preserve the option of future carrier-borne bomber attacks against Japan, President Roosevelt only stated that the planes had flown from "our new secret base at Shangri-La," an allusion to James Hilton's novel *Lost Horizon* and a tongue-in-cheek way of saying to reporters that he would not release the mission's operational details. When the American people learned about the raid, they saw it as both revenge for Pearl Harbor and a sign of the punishment Japan would receive as the war continued. The raid certainly "buoyed the morale of a wounded nation," writes James Scott, just as it was intended to.

One American not celebrating in the immediate aftermath of the raid was Lieutenant Colonel Doolittle. Standing amid the debris of his B-25 strewn across a Chinese mountaintop, he could only wonder how many of his men had survived the mission. Reflecting on the possible deaths of many comrades and the loss of sixteen aircraft, Doolittle told Sergeant Paul Leonard, his crew chief, "I guess they'll court-martial me and send me to prison at Fort Leavenworth."

To the contrary, Doolittle became an instant national hero. General Hap Arnold promoted him to brigadier general, and President Roosevelt presented Doolittle with the Medal of Honor on May 19. At this time, the War Department finally issued a three-page press release and a two-page statement by Doolittle offering the first details of the mission, although leaving out the *Hornet*'s role, the loss of all the bombers and the number of U.S. casualties. The American public was left with the false impression that all of the airmen and planes had made it through safely. Only much later would all the truths of the mission be known, including the fates of the captured Raiders.

In a radio address the next evening, Doolittle offered these perspectives on the raid:

> *No group of men could have thrown themselves into a task more whole-heartedly. They did not seek the path of glory. They merely volunteered for a hazardous mission, knowing full well what such a phrase implied concerning their chances for personal safety. They followed the finest traditions of American fighting men.*
>
> *This was to be no dare-devil, hit-or-miss attack. We planned carefully; we worked long and hard to make our mission a success. The planes themselves—B-25's—were especially equipped for the mission....I bring you this message from Shangri-La: My faith in American fighting men has never been so strong. We have in our training centers, on our production lines, the pattern from which will be built many more surprises for Japan and Germany. It is the ultimate pattern for our own victory.*

Back in Mishawaka, initial news of the Doolittle Raid was received much as it was throughout the country. Because details of the mission were kept secret during production, Ball-Band workers could only suspect that their fuel cells had been used in the raid. According to George Newitt, "Later, when Col. Doolittle was promoted to a brigadier general, the suspicion became stronger because all concerned were well aware of Doolittle's personal interest in the job and his visits to the Mishawaka plant."

Doolittle soon after ended any speculation by sending out congratulatory telegrams to companies that had worked on the B-25s used in the raid. One of these telegrams, dated May 21, 1942, read as follows:

THE EMPLOYEES OF US RUBBER CO.

NOW IT CAN BE TOLD OFFICIALLY: WE BOMBED TOKIO IN THE NORTH AMERICAN BOMBERS YOU HELPED BUILD. EACH PLANE PERFORMED MAGNIFICENTLY, RACING TO ITS OBJECTIVE JUST OVER THE HOUSETOPS, THEN SHOOTING UP A FEW HUNDRED FEET TO DROP ITS BOMBS. OUR PLANES EASILY OUTMANEUVERED THE JAPANESE PURSUIT SHIPS. EVERY BOMB SEEMED TO SMASH INTO ITS TARGET. FLAMES POURED FROM THE ENEMY MILITARY AND NAVAL INSTALLATIONS AND ONE SALVO MADE A DIRECT HIT ON A NEW WARSHIP UNDER CONSTRUCTION. WE FLEW

LOW ENOUGH AT TIMES TO SEE THE SURPRISED LOOK ON FACES IN TOKIO AND OTHER JAPANESE CITIES. EVERY ONE OF THE SEVENTY-NINE MEN ON THE FLIGHT JOIN ME IN PRAISING THE B-TWENTY-FIVE. THE JAP PLANES COULDN'T DO A THING TO STOP US. THEY WILL NEVER STOP US IF YOU KEEP UP YOUR GREAT WORK.

JAMES H. DOOLITTLE, BRIGADIER GENERAL
US ARMY AIR FORCES

The U.S. Rubber Company replied to Doolittle with the following telegram:

THANKS FOR YOUR TELEGRAM AND HEARTIEST CONGRATULATIONS TO YOU AND THE OTHER MEMBERS OF YOUR SQUADRON ON YOUR MARVELOUS ACHIEVEMENT. OUR COMPANY IS GRATIFIED TO HAVE HAD A PART IN THE MANUFACTURE OF THE PLANES WHICH SERVED OUR COUNTRY SO WELL. I KNOW YOUR TELEGRAM WILL BE AN INSPIRATION TO OUR EMPLOYEES TO REDOUBLE THEIR EFFORTS.

F.B. DAVIS, JR. PRESIDENT, UNITED STATES RUBBER COMPANY

In his summary of the fuel cell division's involvement in the Doolittle Raid, George Blair added, "Here again, everybody who participated in this activity got a thrill and a certain satisfaction out of having played even a minor part in this accomplishment."

Sixty-one Doolittle Raiders survived World War II. Starting in 1946, the men began a tradition of annual reunions that included toasting their deceased comrades with special engraved goblets. The last of these official reunions occurred in 2013, when just four of the fliers were still alive. The last surviving Raider, 103-year-old Richard Cole, died in 2019.

Collectively, workers in the Ball-Band fuel cell division were honored on December 26, 1942, when the War Department conferred on the entire plant the Army-Navy Production Award, which recognized excellence in manufacturing war equipment.

The Mishawaka factory that manufactured the fuel tanks that enabled the Doolittle Raiders to bomb Japan and reach China and the Soviet Union continued to make fuel cells for B-25s, B-17s, B-26s, PBM-3s, A20Cs and PT-boats during the war. Fuel tanks were the most prominent of Ball-Band's wartime products, which also included army raincoats, navy deep-sea diving suits and aviator boots.

This former Ball-Band building along North Main Street housed the fuel cell production line and the fuel cell lab. The building, shown here in 1999, was razed in 2000. *Author's collection.*

The Mishawaka Rubber & Woolen Company contracted its name to Mishawaka Rubber Company in 1958, and U.S. Rubber rebranded the plant as Uniroyal in 1967. After Uniroyal filed for bankruptcy in 1990, diminished production continued at the Mishawaka factory until it shut down entirely on April 1, 1997. The building along Main Street that housed the fuel cell production line and lab was razed in 2000 as part of the redevelopment of the former Uniroyal site. No historical marker or monument in Mishawaka specifically refers to Ball-Band's critical role in the Doolittle Raid. The Ball-Band monument on the north bank of the river near the Main Street Bridge, though, briefly tells the factory's story, including three sentences on the production of fuel cells for B-25s, B-26s and PT-boats.

Today, the IronWorks office building stands on the location where Lieutenant Colonel Jimmy Doolittle once inspected the fuel cells being made for the B-25s that he and his men would fly to Tokyo.

The Doolittle Raiders carried out one of the most daring attacks in American military history, an action that would begin to turn the tide of war in the Pacific. The nation has honored their bravery and sacrifice, but our community should also remember the creative, tireless and dedicated Mishawaka factory workers who helped strike this blow for victory against Imperial Japan.

CHAPTER 9

THE MISHAWAKAN WHO SAVED FORD MOTOR COMPANY

Richard Caleal and the 1949 Ford

For a city its size, Mishawaka enjoys a rich automotive tradition. From 1904 to 1915, Simplex Motor Car Company manufactured vehicles in Mishawaka. The company opened a new factory on Byrkit Avenue in 1906, sold its Amplex through a national network of distributors and even entered two cars in the inaugural Indianapolis 500 in 1911. Gillette Motor Company built automobiles in Mishawaka before World War I, and Kenworthy Motors manufactured cars from 1920 to 1922. Mishawaka's AM General plant produced transit buses in the 1970s before it became world-famous for manufacturing the all-terrain military Humvee in the mid-1980s and, later, civilian Hummers and other vehicles.

Another chapter of the Princess City's automotive history has long been overlooked though. It involves Richard Caleal, the kitchen of his home at 317 East Borley Avenue and the car design that saved Ford Motor Company.

Richard David Caleal was born in Lansing, Michigan, on September 2, 1912, the only son of Salim and Mary Caleal, who were Lebanese immigrants. As a boy, Richard developed an affinity for automobiles. "I think I might have been born drawing cars, though my earliest recollection of my love for the automobile is at the age of seven when a dark green Rolls-Royce Silver Ghost drove in front of my house on Cedar Street in Lansing, Michigan," he remembered in a 1993 interview for *Collectible Automobile* magazine. "I ran after it until it disappeared from sight and could think of nothing else after that." Two years later, Caleal began writing to the Rolls-Royce showroom in New York City, asking for pictures of new models, which he would study, trace and modify with his own design ideas. When Richard was older, he also began visiting automobile showrooms in Lansing.

After graduating from high school, Caleal attended Michigan State University. Pursuing his passion for autos, Richard made a one-eighth-size clay model of one of his designs and brought it to Chrysler Corporation in Detroit. The heads of both exterior design and interior design were impressed by the model, and Chrysler offered Richard a job designing car interiors. He turned it down, though, because he was determined to design automobile exteriors.

Unfortunately, the Great Depression made it difficult for Richard to land his preferred job, and he had to settle for

Richard Caleal, 1940s. *Mishawaka Historical Museum.*

working at Quarmby's Wallpaper and Paint, where his duties included selling wallpaper and paint, framing pictures and changing the display windows each week. As Richard dressed the windows, he would include some of his own sketches, which caught the attention of Steven Kish, the foreman at Oldsmobile's Woodshop, who suggested that Caleal meet with John Oswald, head of Body Design. Oswald found the sketches appealing, but no jobs were immediately available.

Richard persisted in his efforts to find a position in automotive design. He moved to Detroit, took a job at the Pan American Paint and Wallpaper Company and began visiting Harry Shaw, chief engineer of R.E.O. Motor Car Company's Body Design Section and later of General Motors' Art and Color, every two weeks to ask about employment. After three months of these inquiries, Shaw gave Caleal a job as a clay modeler and draftsman with the Cadillac Division. When Richard developed eyesight problems, he moved to the sheet metal shop and made prototype models. Richard then worked in styling at Hudson Motor Car Company for a year before taking a position in the Body Division of R.E.O.'s Engineering Department, where he headed a project to design a bus.

While working at R.E.O., Caleal was introduced to a woman from Mishawaka named Margaret Adelaide Arata. Adelaide was seven years younger than Richard, the fifth oldest of Alphonsus and Jennie Arata's nine children. She was a member of Mishawaka High School's class of 1937 and a graduate of the St. Joseph Hospital School of Nursing. The 1942 city directory shows Adelaide living with her parents at 402 East Jefferson Boulevard. She was a nurse employed by the Portage Township trustee and served patients on the poor relief rolls. Later in the war, Adelaide was an industrial nurse for Bendix Corporation in South Bend.

Richard and Adelaide enjoyed their time together in Lansing, and she invited him to visit Mishawaka. As they toured Mishawaka, South Bend and Notre Dame, Richard noticed a sign that said, "Welcome to South Bend—Home of Studebaker." Adelaide drove him to the nearby plant, and Richard went inside to speak with Schuyler Jeffries, the chief engineer of the Truck Division and the brother of one of Caleal's co-workers at R.E.O. Jeffries was impressed by Richard's sketchbook and arranged for him to meet Gene Hartig, Studebaker's chief engineer. Hartig explained that Studebaker had only a small styling department and that the war's onset meant there would be little styling work to do.

"Then he asked me if I knew anything about engines," Caleal recalled. "I told him I didn't know a spark plug from a monkey wrench. After I said that, he got up from his chair and came over and shook my hand and said, 'You're just the kind of person we're looking for. Even though you don't know a damn thing about engines, I'm going to give you a job.'"

Richard became a senior layout man and worked on an engine design for Wright Field in Dayton, Ohio. He and Adelaide were married on November 14, 1942, at St. Monica's Church in Mishawaka. After returning from a short honeymoon in Detroit, the newlyweds resided at 302 East Jefferson, one block west of Adelaide's parents.

Caleal remained with Studebaker for three years before taking a job at Packard's jet engine factory in Toledo, Ohio. Richard spent eight months commuting home to Mishawaka on weekends. Bob Bourke, a Studebaker designer, then invited Caleal to work for Raymond Loewy, whose famous studio had a design contract for the South Bend auto manufacturer. Richard was hired by Loewy in 1943. After Studebaker rejected Loewy's design for the 1947 Champion, he reduced his staff, which led to Caleal being laid off in 1946.

Richard returned to Detroit seeking work and showed his drawings to George Walker, who had a studio that Ford Motor Company had recently given a contract to design the 1949 Ford. Ford desperately needed Walker to produce a successful design, one the company could ride to a return of its glory days as an auto manufacturer. At Ford's peak in the 1920s, it produced 61 percent of all automobiles sold in the United States, including 1.5 million

Model Ts each year. Under stiff competition from Plymouth and Chevrolet, though, Ford's market share had declined to just 20 percent by 1940. When Henry Ford II become president of Ford Motor Company in September 1945, it was reportedly losing $10 million per month. Something had to change if one of America's great manufacturers was to survive. The return of peacetime and the reconversion to civilian automobile manufacturing gave Ford II an opportunity to reinvent his company with innovative procedures, concepts and products.

In an article entitled "1949 Ford: The Car that Saved a Company," Terry Boyce explains that this process had already begun in 1943. The company president, Edsel Ford, and E.T. "Bob" Gregorie, chief stylist, started designing two successors to the 1942 Ford, the last model to roll off the assembly lines before the company retooled for exclusively military production. One of these designs was smaller than the 1942 Ford and the other was larger. Edsel Ford died in May 1943, but those designs continued on the road to production until Ernest Breech was hired by Henry Ford II in June 1946 to oversee the company's modernization efforts. Breech evaluated both models and determined that neither would be satisfactory as Ford's first new postwar model. Harold Youngren, head of design, concurred and, despite a short timeframe, told his designers, "Start from scratch!"

Breech needed to think outside the traditional design process, so, in addition to using his own in-house designers, he turned to George Walker's firm to develop an alternative for Ford II and the company's executives to consider.

These circumstances of desperation and potential opened the door for an unemployed freelance automotive designer from Mishawaka to help save Ford Motor Company. "[Walker] told me if I could come up with a design the powers-that-be would accept, he would give me a job at $50,000 per year," Caleal later explained.

Richard eagerly accepted the opportunity and began working at Walker's studio with Elwood Engel and Joe Oros, who were developing their own design for the 1949 Ford. After a few days alongside Engel and Oros, Caleal told Walker that he was not pleased with their drawings and did not want to continue working with them. "I asked George if he would mind if I went back to Mishawaka and designed the car there, and he said that was fine with him," Richard explained.

In 1945, the Caleals had moved to a small bungalow at 317 East Borley, just across the street from Adelaide's parents and a block and a half south of her brother Lucian at 1616 Division Street.

Richard Caleal designed the 1949 Ford in the kitchen of this house at 317 East Borley Avenue. *Mishawaka Historical Museum.*

Caleal came home and put his drawing table in the dining room. He then told Bob Bourke about the opportunity to design a car for Walker but kept secret the manufacturer for whom it was being developed. Richard asked if Bourke had any extra modeling clay available and wanted to know if Bourke would allow him to use a few clay modelers in the evenings to help with the project. Bourke provided the clay and gave permission for the modelers to moonlight. Caleal hired Joe Thompson and John Lutz. "I made up an armature and we started to model up the car according to my design," he recalled.

Mary Geo Caleal Stephenson, Richard and Adelaide's daughter, offered her account of what the Caleal household was like during the remarkable three weeks in 1946 when automotive history was being made at the corner of East Borley and Division. She wrote the following in *Collectible Automobile*:

> *There were lots of friends, relatives, and colleagues in and out of the kitchen—all excited that Dad had landed such a major project. With only five rooms, the house was small; however, the kitchen was good-sized. Dad*

135

pushed the table into the middle of the room so the modelers could work around it. The prints and drawing board were in the dining room, where the overflow of people usually stood, drank coffee, and chatted excitedly as Dad's model took shape.

The result of these efforts was a quarter-scale clay model that Richard later described as "a beautiful thing" and "a sweet-looking job." To get the model to Detroit, Caleal borrowed his sister-in-law's 1935 Ford, removed the right front seat and put the model on the floor. When Richard arrived at Walker's studio, he showed the model to Walker, who, he remembered, "loved it" and "offered glowing approval."

Caleal's design was distinguished by its uninterrupted "slab sides" that eliminated the side fenders found on earlier models, making the fenders and body sides into the same structure. The rear fender came up nearly to the top of the trunk, and the front fender almost reached the hood. There was no fender slope toward the front or rear of the car. The side molding had a line of stainless steel that ran from just behind the front wheel, over the rear wheel cutout, almost to the rear of the car. Caleal's original model had a front grille with a sculpted bar bearing the word *Ford*, but this was later replaced with a spinner grille, which had the look of an aircraft's nose.

Caleal then brought the model back to Mishawaka and made a plaster cast, which would be presented along with the other 1949 Ford candidates to the Ford Operating Committee two weeks later. Richard asked Bob Koto to help with the cast, and they sandpapered the model before taking it to a shop, where Caleal paid twenty-five dollars to have it painted Capri blue. Adelaide went to Robertson's Department Store in South Bend and bought a piece of blue velvet, which she attached to a three-fourth-inch plywood board to make the platform on which the model would rest.

The day before the December 11 presentation, Richard brought the model to Detroit in his father-in-law's 1938 Studebaker. Henry Ford II and his team of executives met at Walker's studio at 8:00 a.m. the next day. Richard later explained what happened next:

At eight o'clock sharp, Ernie Breech, Henry Ford II, Benson Ford, Harold Youngren, Mead Bricker, John Bugas, and Jack Davis arrived. They entered the studio where the three models of the proposed '49 Ford were displayed—one joint model by Joe Oros and Elwood Engel, one by E.T. "Bob" Gregorie, head of Ford styling at that time, and my model. They were in the room a total of approximately four or five minutes when Walker

1949 Ford. *Mishawaka Historical Museum.*

rushed out, threw his arms around me, handed me a Corona (which he smoked at the time), and said, "Dick, they picked your model! I'm going to see you get that job at $50,000 per year."

Ford Motor Company brought Caleal's design into production with some changes. Based on Ford II's recommendation, Engel rotated the taillights from vertical to horizontal. To give the front grille a more engaging look, Oros added the spinner grille in place of Caleal's sculpted bar. Oros and Engel also raised the roofline to create additional headroom. In a 2005 article for *Hemmings Classic Car*, Tim Howley noted that many Ford stylists and clay modelers were also involved with the 1949 Ford before it went into production, designing details such as the hubcaps, hood ornament, front bumper and interior elements.

The 1949 Ford was modified into several versions, including two- and four-door sedans, business and club coupes, a convertible and a station wagon. It sold from between $1,300 and $2,300.

For the car's debut, Ford Motor Company took the 1949 Ford to New York City and rented the Waldorf Astoria's Grand Ballroom from June 10 to June

16, 1948. The media and celebrities were invited to a special showing on June 10. "Everyone who was anyone was there," wrote Stephenson, "including the complete Social Register. Champagne flowed from six bars." The public exhibition began the following day and became a stunning success. The *New York Times* reported that 250,000 people attended the exhibition, and *Business Week* estimated that several hundred thousand came.

Ford spent more than $500,000 on the exhibition, $10 million to advertise its new signature vehicle and $72 million for the equipment needed to manufacture the 1949 Ford. All this investment paid off handsomely for Ford Motor Company, which sold 1,118,308 cars in 1949, more than double the previous year's total of 430,198. "The new Fords sold like hotcakes," wrote Stephenson, "and the life they pumped into Ford not only saved the company but rejuvenated the entire automotive industry." By 1955, Ford had made a record annual profit of $437 million and had increased its market share to 28 percent.

Among the dignitaries and Ford executives who attended the soiree at the Waldorf, one might expect that Richard Caleal would have been the man of the hour, lauded by the automotive world. But that was not to be.

The caption of this news photo from June 1948 announced the New York City exhibition where the 1949 Ford made its debut. *Mishawaka Historical Museum.*

Ford Motor Company spent millions advertising its 1949 models, including color brochures. *Mishawaka Historical Museum.*

Caleal did not even attend the New York exhibition, and his vital role in designing the 1949 Ford was already being downplayed, even hidden, delaying for decades the full story being told. George Walker, though, was there to take credit for the design that his studio had delivered to Ford Motor Company.

Mary Geo Stephenson believes that Walker "deserves some credit for the '49 Ford" because his studio had the contract to design the car and he gave Richard the opportunity to work on the project. It was also standard practice for studio heads to take full credit for the work done by their employees. She noted that Walker did subsequently give Caleal a job as head of advanced styling at Ford Motor Company, although not at the promised $50,000 per year salary. Stephenson asserted, "Walker made a lot of promises to Dad, if only Dad would keep the story under wraps.... My dad did, in fact, keep his word and acquiesced to Walker's wishes for many years."

Richard later admitted his error in keeping the truth to himself: "Looking back, I realize I should have spoken up and taken credit for my design, Walker's wishes notwithstanding." Caleal remembered Youngren, later

Ford Motor Company's vice-president of engineering, and John Oswald, chief body engineer, once asking him for the identity of the real designer of the 1949 Ford. "I told them Walker designed it, which I now realize was a mistake on my part. However, I was working for Walker at the time, and I didn't want to stir things up, and I had made a promise to Walker."

Others were more willing to take credit for the 1949 Ford. In an April 1982 article in *Car Collector* magazine entitled "Walker's Peak, the 1949 Ford," George Walker said, "I would like to be remembered for the 1949 Ford, the car that took a company that was losing $80 million a month and turning it into $80 million monthly profit."

Former Studebaker designer Bob Bourke wrote a book, which included a chapter on the 1949 Ford. Bourke gave himself and Bob Koto all of the credit for the design. According to Caleal, Bourke's version of events is "full of inaccuracies and untruths," including the assertion that Bourke was responsible for the 1949 Ford's spinner grille. Richard's original design had no spinner grille. When Walker found out that new G.M. models included a spinner, he told Oros and Engel to add the spinner to Caleal's design. Richard noted that Bourke deserves credit for putting a spinner grille on Studebaker cars in those years but played no role in its inclusion on the 1949 Ford. Richard also added that Bourke frequently stopped by East Borley during the three-week period in which the design was being made in the Caleals' kitchen. Bourke would offer observations on the design, have some coffee and visit for a while. "Other than giving me a great deal of encouragement, that was it," Richard stated. Bourke's account also gave Koto a significant role in designing the 1949 Ford. In a magazine article, Koto claimed that he designed the car and assisted Caleal with making the mold and cast. Caleal objected to their interpretation of Koto's role: "The truth of the matter is that I hired Koto to help me make the plaster cast and that is all he did. He had nothing to do with my design."

Gradually, though, the truth about the 1949 Ford's origins began to emerge in the 1980s and early 1990s. For forty years, Richard Caleal had kept the model mold for the 1949 Ford in his garage. In 1986, he donated the valuable artifact to the Henry Ford Museum in Dearborn, Michigan. Richard Wright, an automotive reporter for the *Detroit News*, was among the first to credit Caleal with the design after he interviewed Gordon Buehrig, a clay modeler who worked with Caleal, Bourke and Koto at Studebaker. Richard Langworth, who wrote books for *Consumer Guide*, also attributed the design to Caleal. Not until the *Collectible Automobile* article in June 1993, though, did Richard Caleal publicly tell his story. Ford

Motor Company honored Caleal when its Forty-Nine concept car, which was inspired by Caleal's 1949 Ford design, made its debut at the 2001 New York Auto Show. Caleal, then eighty-nine years old, was invited to the press conference. "It's very flattering," he told the *New York Daily News*. "It's like the original—plain and simple."

Caleal's interview and the accompanying narrative by his daughter were not the last word on the controversy and mystery surrounding who designed the 1949 Ford. As Tim Howley wrote, "But here is where the story moves into the Twilight Zone." Howley stated that he had trouble believing that Caleal and a few moonlighters could create "such a revolutionary design and model it in just three weeks," and he began to suspect that something had happened at Studebaker that facilitated Caleal's design. Around 2003, Howley found five photos in California labeled "1946 Studebaker Champion Project," which included one showing a model that "is nearly a dead ringer for the 1949 Ford club coupe." Intrigued, he decided to investigate further by reading Studebaker design articles from the 1940s and talking with stylists of that era. Based on this research, Howley was able to piece together what he thinks is "a probable other half of the story of how the 1949 Ford design may have originated."

The models in the photographs were made by Raymond Loewy's design staff working for Studebaker. These stylists included Bourke, Koto, Buehrig and several others, including Caleal. Howley speculated, "The purest 1949 Ford as a Studebaker was probably designed primarily by Holden Koto and Bob Bourke." Virgil Exner, Studebaker's head of styling, stated in a 1973 article that Studebaker built a full-scale wooden mock-up, which he described as a "flush-sided job," a reference to the slab-sided appearance that would later distinguish the 1949 Ford. Exner explained that this mock-up convinced him that Studebaker's "first post-war car shouldn't be completely flush-sided," which Howley interprets to mean "that anything along the lines of the '49 Ford was never going to fly at Studebaker." Exner did not like Loewy, and this feeling was shared by the head of engineering, Roy Cole, who encouraged Exner to make his own alternative design, which was eventually chosen over the one made by Loewy's team.

As this version of the 1947 Studebaker Champion was readied for production, Loewy had to reduce his Studebaker design personnel. Among the designers he let go was Richard Caleal. Howley explained what happened next: "Caleal was very well-liked, and everybody was sorry to see him leave. They were all delighted to help him out when he got the assignment from George Walker. Nobody but Caleal had a clue this was to be for Ford. But it would take nothing short of a miracle to produce something acceptable in three weeks. So they may have gone back to a design that was abandoned at Studebaker, the slab-sided coupe."

Howley acknowledged that it has long been rumored that the 1947 Studebaker design that most resembled the 1949 Ford was the one made by Loewy's designers and passed over in favor of the Exner design. He shared a related rumor that the Loewy designers were so angry that they "gave this very design to Caleal and redid it on Caleal's kitchen table. So the 1949 Ford was designed more out of spite than anything else." None of Loewy's designers could publicly take credit for the 1949 Ford because Loewy would have fired them for giving Caleal a rejected Studebaker design. According to this account, Loewy's men were pleased to let Caleal have the acclaim for what they had done.

Howley concluded that "it is totally possible that Studebaker's abandoned design became the car that saved the Ford Motor Company and ushered in a whole new era in automotive design." He also suggested that top Ford executives engaged in a "massive cover-up" of the real origins of the 1949 Ford because "the full story would have been a major embarrassment to the company."

Richard Caleal continued as Ford's head of advanced styling until Chrysler offered to make him head of the Dodge Truck Studio and promised to later make him vice-president of styling. Caleal never received the latter position, though, and was demoted by Virgil Exner when he became vice-president of styling. When Exner retired, Elwood Engel replaced him. According to Mary Geo Stephenson, George Walker visited Engel's studio and suggested that he "get rid of Dick." She suggested that Engel's receptiveness to firing Caleal resulted from knowing the truth about the 1949 Ford. When Richard learned that he was about to be dismissed, he found a position as an engineer in body ornamentation. He later worked his way back up to executive status with Chrysler.

Stephenson remembered that the Caleal home in Detroit "was always open to young designers." They would often come for dinner and then stay to work on design projects. Caleal helped many of these designers find jobs at Detroit auto manufacturers.

Richard Caleal died on September 16, 2006, in West Bloomfield, Michigan. He was ninety-four years old and survived by his wife of nearly sixty-four years, their daughter and sons Richard Jr. and Daniel. Richard is buried with Adelaide and her family at St. Joseph Cemetery in Mishawaka, just half a mile west of the house where he made automotive history in

Richard and Adelaide are shown with their children—Richard Jr., Mary Geo and Daniel— in the 1950s. *Mishawaka Historical Museum.*

1946. Caleal's gravestone bears a simple but unique epitaph: "American Automotive Designer."

While he lived long enough to enjoy some recognition for his role in designing the 1949 Ford, Richard received his greatest honor posthumously. On October 6, 2009, he was inducted into the American Automotive Hall of Fame in Dearborn, Michigan.

The streets of Mishawaka are lined with thousands of houses, each with its own history. For some, their significance has been recognized through newspaper articles or even a few historical markers. More often, though, their stories have been remembered only by the people who resided in these homes. For decades, the house at 317 East Borley, seemingly indistinguishable from others in its neighborhood, has stood as a silent witness to the automotive history made within its walls by Richard Caleal and the 1949 Ford.

MISHAWAKA STRIKES BACK

Bendix's Talos Missile and the Vietnam War

The history of warfare is full of complex cause-and-effect relationships and compelling ironies. One such set of remarkable circumstances involves the two most prominent topics from Mishawaka's Vietnam War years: the Talos surface-to-air missile (SAM) and U.S. Air Force captain Richard C. Brenneman.

On November 8, 1967, Brenneman, a Mishawaka native, was shot down while flying his F-4 Phantom jet on a combat mission near Hanoi, North Vietnam. He was captured and spent 1,954 days as a prisoner of war until his release in March 1973.

The Brenneman family home at 1801 East Third Street was just two blocks north of the factory where Bendix Corporation manufactured Talos missiles for the U.S. Navy. Through Captain Brenneman and the Talos, this East End neighborhood was tied closely to the Vietnam War.

On May 23, 1968, six months after one of its sons had become a casualty in the skies over North Vietnam, Mishawaka would strike back. On that day and several subsequent occasions, the Talos would be an instrument of vengeance against the North Vietnamese military.

The story of Mishawaka's Talos missile begins in World War II as the major combatants sought to develop missiles that could destroy enemy ships. The United States started its anti-ship missile program in 1940 and was able to use radar-guided missiles to sink Japanese ships before the war's end.

With the Japanese also attempting to produce missiles capable of destroying Allied vessels, the U.S. Navy correctly predicted that anti-ship missiles would become the greatest threat to the fleet in the years ahead. Before Japan could deploy anti-ship missile technology, it began using the more conventional, but still deadly, kamikaze planes in October 1944.

Just as these attacks were beginning, the Navy Bureau of Ordinance (BuOrd) approached the Johns Hopkins Applied Physics Laboratory (APL) in the fall of 1944, seeking assistance with weapons systems to protect its ships against enemy aircraft and missiles. On December 1, 1944, BuOrd and APL entered into a contract to create an interceptor missile to counter the threat to surface vessels. This secret project became known as "Bumblebee."

In early 1945, APL asked the Bendix Products Division in South Bend to build the fuel regulators for ramjet test vehicles. Twelve Bendix employees were initially part of Project Bumblebee, and that number grew as larger missiles were constructed. At first, Bendix's missile development work was done near its Brake and Steering Division in South Bend. The expanding operations required larger facilities, though, so Bendix purchased a seven-acre property at 400 South Beiger Street in Mishawaka in April 1951.

This site had already played a prominent role in the history of Mishawaka industry, but its greatest part would come through Bendix and the Talos. In 1900, Herman Romunder developed the first waterproof glue and started producing laminated bent wood cases in a building east of the Ball-Band plant. The next year, the National Veneer Products Company began manufacturing large steamer trunks featuring wood veneer, the patented glue and metal trim and locks. Tremendous demand for the Indestructo trunks led Romunder to soon move production to South Beiger. National Veneer Products trunks were regarded as the best on the market, known for withstanding rigorous tests of their durability. The firm rebranded as the Indestructo Trunk Company in 1913. During World War I, Indestructo manufactured De Havilland DH.4 aircraft fuselages and wing forms for the War Department. After production of trunks resumed in 1919, Indestructo prospered until the Great Depression all but wiped out demand for its luggage, and the business entered receivership in 1935. The factory was purchased in 1936 by the Paramount Furniture Company, which remained there until 1949.

The navy's new missile needed a name, and "Talos" (pronounced with a long *a* and long *o*) was selected in January 1948. Talos was an ancient Greek demigod who defended the island of Crete by flying at a speed so great that he became red hot. He seized his enemies, pressed them close to his chest and burned them up. For a supersonic missile system that would be tasked with defending the fleet, it was the perfect appellation.

Bendix continued its development of the Talos in the 1950s. Tactical Talos missiles were first tested at White Sands Missile Range in 1955 and installed on the cruiser USS *Galveston* in 1958. The Talos missiles were twenty-one feet long, had a diameter of twenty-eight inches and weighed 3,360 pounds. An additional eleven-foot long, 4,360-pound solid rocket booster accelerated the missile to a speed of Mach 2.5 and was jettisoned when the missile reached its cruising speed. At that point, the ramjet engine propelled the missile to its target. In contrast to turbojets, which used a turbine and compressor for fuel combustion, the Talos's ramjet engine employed the missile's motion to compress the air entering at the front. The forty-thousand-horsepower Talos engine used only one-sixth to one-eighth of the fuel that a rocket would have needed for similar thrust.

In addition to its revolutionary ramjet, the Talos used two "brain systems" to guide the missile to its target. A guidance beam from the launching ship led the Talos to the target area, using information from different radars. At the end of the beam-riding phase of flight, the ship sent a signal to arm the warhead and switch control from the "beam brain" to the "homing brain." The launching ship painted the target with a homing signal that registered with the missile's semi-active radar homing seeker and directed the missile to its target. The accuracy of the terminal homing system was thus not influenced by the ship's distance from the target. The warhead then detonated when it came within "kill range." The Talos's guidance system allowed it to fly with greater fuel efficiency, according to retired naval officer Phillip Hays: "The missile did not end up in a long, circuitous fuel-consuming tail chase as it approached the target. Instead, the missile was guided to an altitude where it operated efficiently, and it was then flown to a predicted intercept point ahead of the target….In the final phase of the intercept, the missile dove on the target from above." Talos missiles could fly as high as eighty thousand feet, an altitude greater than any enemy bomber was capable of.

Because the ramjet required a large air intake at the front of the missile, the usual way of placing a radar seeker—a parabolic antenna—could not be used because it would disrupt the air intake. Instead, four antennas were placed around the air intake, an arrangement that would not obstruct the ramjet's airflow. These small antennas facilitated the missile's acquisition of a target without having to be fed information from the launching ship. The air intake and four antennas gave the Talos its distinctive appearance, which was augmented by three sets of four short wings or fins.

The Talos's payload was a 465-pound warhead, either conventional or nuclear.

This interior view of the Bendix plant in Mishawaka shows Talos missiles being assembled. *Mishawaka-Penn-Harris Public Library.*

A "Talos Fact Sheet" published by Bendix's Mishawaka Division in 1959 proudly reported that "many 'firsts' have resulted from its program of development," including "an advanced version of the first ram-jet engine; new records in the size and development of solid-fuel booster rockets; first flights of fully controlled missile powered by ram-jet engines; first to employ a dual-guidance system with precise accuracy at short and long ranges; and pioneering steps in the introduction of warheads with atomic capabilities." Talos was also the first missile to bear a tactical nuclear weapon.

Admiral Arleigh Burke, chief of naval operations, described the Talos as the "best [anti-aircraft] missile in any arsenal in the world."

The Talos was not without its flaws. Talos missiles required significant maintenance and a large amount of space on board the ships where they were deployed. Hays noted that a battery in the missile needed to be changed monthly and that each Talos required testing every two months. The Talos system was able to track only six targets at one time and could engage just two targets simultaneously, leaving the fleet vulnerable "to saturation attacks

Bendix used this mobile Missile Test Laboratory, which advertised Mishawaka's unique role in one of the U.S. Navy's most advanced weapons systems. *Mishawaka-Penn-Harris Public Library.*

by large numbers of aircraft." The Talos's other detriments included a sluggish response time and a substantial minimum distance for engaging the enemy, which made the missile less effective against closer targets that suddenly appeared on the ship's radar screens.

Bendix's South Beiger Street factory underwent transformation as Talos production ramped up in the 1950s. The federal government bought 60.6 acres adjacent to the old furniture factory in 1952 and constructed an Environmental Test building—described by Bendix as "the most complete test laboratory of its kind in the world"—in 1953. Subsequent expansion at the plant included a state-of-the-art, 100,000-square-foot manufacturing building (1954), an engineering building (1956), a manufacturing building addition (1958) and storage buildings (1960). At the peak of Talos production in the late 1950s and early 1960s, Bendix employed 1,850 people at its Mishawaka facility.

The Talos was designed as "the long-range fist of the fleet," and its launch platform was the guided missile cruisers *Galveston* (commissioned 1958), *Little Rock* (1960), *Oklahoma City* (1960), *Long Beach* (1961), *Albany* (1962), *Columbus* (1962) and *Chicago* (1964). The three older cruisers each carried one Mk-7

Mishawakans got their first glimpse of the Talos missile during the 1958 Memorial Day Parade. *Mishawaka-Penn-Harris Public Library.*

Guided Missile Launching System twin launcher and 46 Talos missiles, *Long Beach* had a Mk-12 twin launcher and 52 Talos missiles and the three *Albany*-class cruisers were each armed with two Mk-12 twin launchers and 104 Talos missiles. On February 24, 1959, *Galveston* fired the first Talos missile at sea. The first ship-launched Talos to destroy a drone was fired by *Little Rock* on October 21, 1960. The range of Talos missiles was kept classified during their years of active service, but *Chicago* downed a drone at ninety-six miles—the longest-range Talos kill recorded—in July 1967.

Of these seven vessels equipped with Talos missiles, *Long Beach* was the only cruiser specifically designed for carrying Talos missiles. In addition, it was equipped with Terrier surface-to-air missiles, which had a range of roughly twenty miles. After initial service in the Atlantic Fleet, the cruiser was transferred to the Pacific and sent to Vietnam in 1966–69 and 1972–73.

In *Black Shoes and Blue Water*, Malcolm Muir Jr. explained that the Talos would have seen combat in Vietnam sooner if Admiral U.S. Grant Sharp, the commander-in-chief of Pacific naval forces (CINCPAC), had had his way. As early as 1966, Sharp had unsuccessfully lobbied the Joint Chiefs of Staff (JCS) to allow Talos missiles to be fired at MiGs over North Vietnam and

Talos missiles on the deck of the cruiser USS *Little Rock*. *U.S. Navy.*

not just used for fleet defense. The JCS repeatedly denied these entreaties, fearing that a Talos might fall into enemy hands, strike a U.S. plane or cause North Vietnamese civilian deaths. Such a restriction was one of many ways that the American military fought the Vietnam War with one hand tied behind its back.

Long Beach left its home port of Long Beach, California, on November 7, 1966, and arrived in the northern Gulf of Tonkin, 30 miles off Haiphong, North Vietnam, on November 30. Equipped with the Naval Tactical Data System (NTDS), it was a PIRAZ (Positive Identification Radar Advisory Zone) ship, tasked with identifying and tracking all aircraft within its radar coverage area, directing U.S. fighters to engage North Vietnamese MiGs, aiding search and rescue efforts and alerting American pilots who approached Chinese territory. Had the American aircraft carriers and other ships at Yankee Station, 100 miles south of PIRAZ Station and 150 miles east of Da Nang, been attacked by North Vietnamese aircraft, *Long Beach* was at the ready to alert the fleet and use its complement of Talos missiles to shoot down the bogies. In fact, MiGs would sometimes fly at high speed over the water toward U.S. vessels and then veer off before the Americans would take defensive action. A destroyer typically accompanied PIRAZ cruisers to defend against a torpedo boat attack. *Long Beach* continued at PIRAZ Station until April 1967 and returned to the West Coast on July 4.

Long Beach's second tour of duty in the Far East began in April 1968 and would prove more memorable and historic. The cruiser was again at PIRAZ Station, rotating with a guided missile frigate, each serving in this capacity for a month. According to a former combat information center crew member of a U.S. vessel stationed in the area, the North Vietnamese Air Force seemed to know which ship was patrolling the waters. When *Long Beach* was on patrol, the North Vietnamese MiGs would stay farther inland, aware that the ship's Talos missiles had greater range than the frigate's Terriers.

After having tracked more than five hundred MiGs, *Long Beach* at last received the go-ahead to fire its Talos at enemy fighters. On May 11, the cruiser launched Talos missiles at North Vietnamese MiGs in what Norman Polmar and Edward Marolda refer to as "the first—albeit unsuccessful—U.S. attempt to down hostile aircraft with surface-to-air missiles." They note that five different times during that month North Vietnamese aircraft attempted to attack U.S. Navy vessels.

Long Beach would soon get a shot at redemption and more naval warfare history. *Long Beach* completed thirty-five days of PIRAZ duty, and a frigate moved north to replace it. After the two ships exchanged much deliberate radio chatter about *Long Beach* heading to Australia, the cruiser steamed south past the aircraft carriers at Yankee Station. During the night, though, *Long Beach* masked its radar emissions, turned around and headed back toward PIRAZ Station and the frigate. *Long Beach* positioned itself so close to the

On May 23, 1968, a Talos missile shot down a North Vietnamese MiG-21 like this one. *Mishawaka Historical Museum.*

frigate that they appeared to have a single radar image. Sailors were told to avoid radio references to *Long Beach*'s presence in the area.

The next day, May 23, the North Vietnamese moved a group of MiG-21 fighters from a base west of Hanoi toward Haiphong, apparently assuming that they only needed to stay more than thirty miles from the PIRAZ frigate to be safe from its Terrier missiles. U.S. vessels with long-range radar identified the aircraft and relayed the information to the NTDS. *Long Beach* then fired two Talos RIM-8 missiles, two minutes apart, one of which shot down a MiG at a range of sixty-five miles. A second MiG, reports another source, was destroyed as it flew through the debris from the first.

CINCPAC offered this account of the engagement: "Two minutes and 50 seconds [after the first missile was fired] all of Talos directors recorded on their scopes the sudden blooming and the expanding clutter of debris associated with a direct hit. At the same instant, electronics signals from the MiG abruptly stopped. Two minutes later, the second Talos detonated on the falling wreckage."

Long Beach and the Talos had scored the first-ever kill of a hostile aircraft by a ship-fired missile and, noted Muir, "the first time that a nuclear surface warship had scored against an enemy." Although neither Captain

Brenneman nor anyone on the cruiser could have known it, the tortured and suffering POW had been avenged by a missile made within sight of his backyard in far-off Mishawaka.

Continuing its PIRAZ responsibilities in the summer and fall, *Long Beach* used a Talos to shoot down another MiG in September at a distance of sixty-one miles.

Noting *Long Beach*'s success, Vice Admiral Gerald Miller, who occasionally visited the ship on PIRAZ duty, commented, "I've always said that if we could get it [a MiG] with Talos, why the hell are we going to put a guy [in a plane] over the beach up there and jeopardize him getting shot down?"

The Talos was not perfect in combat conditions, though. On five occasions, *Long Beach* had fired Talos missiles and not scored a hit. Guidance radars from the missiles could be detected by North Vietnamese shore facilities, which warned aircraft to dive and fly low or behind hills to evade the missiles.

In the fall of 1968, JCS ordered an end to the practice of firing Talos missiles over land, limiting their use only to the Gulf of Tonkin. Naval personnel were frustrated by this self-imposed handicap, and their view was later affirmed by Admiral Sharp: "Thus we denied ourselves an excellent weapon which could have made life very difficult for the MiGs over North Vietnam. *Long Beach* and her Talos missiles were perfectly capable of intercepting a MiG aircraft over the Hanoi-Haiphong area, and their accuracy was very good indeed."

After the bombing of North Vietnam resumed later in the war, JCS changed this policy, and the Talos was again used to directly facilitate the American air campaign.

As part of that effort, the Talos proved also to be an effective surface-to-surface missile to counter North Vietnamese use of mobile radar units. U.S. forces had obliterated every fixed radar installation in North Vietnam, so the enemy employed Russian-built radar trucks that could coordinate fighter attacks and SAM launches against U.S. bombers. The Defense Department needed a way to destroy these mobile units by long-range attack, and it turned to the Talos RGM-8H anti-radiation missile (ARM), which had a 120-mile range.

USS *Oklahoma City* was equipped with the classified RGM-8H in the spring of 1971. As the North Vietnamese prepared for a February 1972 offensive, they relocated missiles, aircraft and mobile radar units closer to the DMZ to support the attack. U.S. Air Force radar suppression aircraft had to get within thirty miles to fire at the mobile units, which limited the attacks' effectiveness.

In January 1972, *Oklahoma City* moved into the Gulf of Tonkin, tasked with taking out a radar unit near Mu Gia Pass. From January 28 to February 4, the ship held its position thirty miles off shore. USS *Chicago* was also in the area on "radar-hunting" duty.

On February 3, *Chicago* fired a Talos ARM at a North Vietnamese radar truck, but mechanical problems with the rear telemetry unit caused the missile to fail mid-flight. The next evening, *Chicago* fired another RGM-8H, and it also failed from an undetermined cause.

Around 2100 on February 4, *Oklahoma City* detected an air traffic control radar, and then "the fun started," in the words of Phillip Hays, who was then a nuclear/special weapons officer on board the cruiser. Over the next few hours, electronics warfare (EW) personnel monitored the North Vietnamese signal and sent the frequency information to fire control while a Talos was readied for launch. Doug Rasor, working EW that night, recalled what happened next: "I continued to monitor the signal as the missile was in-flight. After a minute or so, I remember hearing a weird screeching… then the signal went silent. Apparently that was the precise moment of the impact/explosion that 'killed' the radar."

A Talos missile launches from the USS *Oklahoma City*. *U.S. Navy.*

Hays described what aerial reconnaissance photos showed the next day: "The radar antennas were scattered all over Southeast Asia, and what remained of the trailer was lying on its side at the edge of a 30-foot diameter crater."

Oklahoma City and its Talos missile had made history: the U.S. Navy's first successful combat surface-to-surface missile firing and anti-radiation missile attack. The operation was classified, and missile crewmen were ordered not to speak of it. Nonetheless, word of *Oklahoma City*'s achievement soon spread throughout Southeast Asia. Malcolm Muir Jr. reported that the Talos ARM's presence once caused the North Vietnamese to close down their radar facilities for a full week.

Mishawaka's Talos missile added one more MiG kill to its Vietnam War record on May 9, 1972. A Talos fired from *Chicago* destroyed a MiG at a range of forty-eight miles, causing other attacking MiGs to turn tail and flee. The cruiser also launched four Talos RIM-8H against North Vietnamese radar units.

When American participation in the Vietnam War concluded in January 1973, the Talos missile's days of active duty for fleet defense were numbered, and the navy began phasing it out in 1974. The Talos itself was still an effective weapon, but its launch platform—the seven cruisers—was becoming obsolete, and no other ship was large enough to carry Talos missiles. *Galveston* was decommissioned in 1970, followed by *Columbus* (1975), *Little Rock* (1976), *Oklahoma City* (1979), *Chicago* (1980) and *Albany* (1980). On November 6, 1979, *Oklahoma City* fired the last ship-launched Talos missile. *Long Beach* had its Talos missiles removed in 1979 and sailed on with Standard, Harpoon and Tomahawk missiles until it was decommissioned in 1995.

All told, the Bendix plant in Mishawaka manufactured 2,404 Talos missiles, and 1,349 of these were fired in combat or practice between 1958 and 1979. In 1960s dollars, the Talos reportedly cost $386,000 each, which amounts to $1 billion for the missiles' full production run. This might seem a steep price for shooting down three or four MiGs and destroying one mobile radar unit during the Vietnam War. What will never be fully known or quantified, though, is the deterrent effect of the Talos. Without this missile system guarding U.S. vessels off the coast of Vietnam, MiGs might have judged attacks against the fleet to be less risky, thus endangering thousands of American sailors, imperiling their expensive ships and interfering with flight operations on aircraft carriers at Yankee Station.

The Talos weapons system had officially come to an end when the last missiles were offloaded from *Long Beach*, *Oklahoma City*, *Chicago* and *Albany*.

Even before this, plans were underway for the remaining Talos stock to serve a new purpose: supersonic target drones. After the last Talos was taken out of service, the unused missiles were converted into Vandal drones at the Bendix facility in Mishawaka.

The Vandal was a modified version of the Talos. The missile's guidance system and air intake were altered so the Vandal could fly supersonic at low altitudes, similar to an anti-ship missile. The Vandal carried more fuel and was four feet longer than the Talos. Its maximum cruising speed was Mach 2.2, and it had a range of 43.5 miles. Launchers from decommissioned Talos ships were used to fire Vandals from land-based platforms. The first of 644 Vandals was launched in 1977, and the program continued until the available missiles were used up in 2005.

Back in Mishawaka, the South Beiger Street plant stayed busy, albeit with much-diminished employment levels, converting the old Talos missiles into Vandals. During the 1980s and 1990s, the innovative engineers at AlliedSignal Aerospace Target Systems, as the plant was known after Bendix merged in 1982, made many modifications to the missile's equipment and advancements in its performance.

The large Talos missile plant was no longer needed for the Vandal, so Bendix downsized its facility in 1979, moving to the Bendix Building, located at the north end of the property. That same year, Elkhart-based Miles Laboratories bought the former navy building and Talos plant.

In the late 1990s, AlliedSignal's Target Systems Division still employed 150 people in Mishawaka. When the U.S. Navy considered switching to a new supersonic target drone, AlliedSignal proposed the Sea Snake, which would have been produced at the Mishawaka plant. The navy later rejected the Sea Snake and chose not to continue the Vandal program. As a result, all missile production in Mishawaka ceased in 2000. The former Talos plant bought by Miles still stands and is where Ascensia Diabetes Care now manufactures its blood glucose monitoring system. The building that AlliedSignal used for the Vandal sat vacant for more than a decade before it was demolished in 2012. All that remains of the historic structure is the concrete pad that was once the floor on which technicians made the Vandal missiles.

Although the Talos flies no more, a few surviving missiles can be visited at museums around the country. A Talos also hangs in the atrium of the South Bend Airport, and two of the missiles are featured in the adjacent Military Honor Park. Perhaps someday a Talos will come home for display in Mishawaka.

Over the past 160 years, the Princess City has manufactured a variety of products for the armed forces, including Milburn wagons, Ball-Band fuel cells, Dodge ship propulsion systems and AM General Humvees. Most extraordinary of all, though, were Bendix's Talos missiles, through which the might of Mishawaka industry influenced strategy and tactics in the Vietnam War and brought retribution to the nation's enemies.

ABOUT THE AUTHOR

P eter J. De Kever is a lifelong Mishawaka resident and the city's historian laureate. He has written several books that teach about and celebrate Mishawaka's historical identity.